# The Buddha in Everyone's Heart

# The Buddha in Everyone's Heart
*Seeking the World of the Lotus Sutra*

Kosho Niwano

*translated by*
Margaret Suzuki *and* Richard Look

*with a foreword by*
Miriam Levering

Kosei Publishing Co. • Tokyo

This book was originally published in Japanese by Kosei Publishing Co. under the title *Kaiso-sama ni Naraite.*

Editing by William Feuillan and DeAnna Satre.

Cover design by Abinitio Design.

First English edition, 2013

Published by Kosei Publishing Co., Kosei Building, 2-7-1 Wada, Suginami-ku, Tokyo 166-8535, Japan. Copyright © 2013 by Kosei Publishing Co.; all rights reserved. Printed in Japan.

ISBN 978-4-333-02552-7

# Contents

I once saw the founder in an unforgettable posture.
In our home, after the daily sutra recitations,
Just as the family were getting to their feet,
A view of the founder from behind:
One lone man in deep, really deep, reverence before the home altar,
Both palms flat on the floor and face down.
This view of him should have been very familiar to us in the family,
But to me then, looking at him from behind made my spirit tremble
To think of the sacredness of the moments shared
Between the gods and the buddhas and those who have absolute trust in them.
And I thought that the starting point of the founder's single-minded journey
Along the one path of his faith was distilled in this view of him from behind.
I really wanted to understand then about his belief in the Lotus Sutra,
How he viewed this world of ours, and the essence of what he wanted to teach us.
And I wondered if I, too, could see the world of the Buddha as he saw it.
Those were my thoughts then.

Kosho Niwano

# FOREWORD

This is a remarkable book by one Buddhist teacher about another. The author, Kosho Niwano, is a wife and mother, now in her forties. She is also a Buddhist leader who is preparing to assume the presidency of one of the largest Buddhist movements in the world, Rissho Kosei-kai.

Rissho Kosei-kai is composed entirely of Buddhist laypeople like Kosho herself, not monks and nuns. It was founded in Tokyo in 1938 by Kosho Niwano's grandfather, Nikkyo Niwano. He remained the president of Rissho Kosei-kai until he was succeeded by his eldest son, Nichiko Niwano, several years before his death in 1999 at the age of ninety-two. Rissho Kosei-kai is heir to the teachings of the Buddha, transmitted over a period of two and a half millennia from India to China and Korea, and then to Japan. For Rissho Kosei-kai members, the Buddha's teachings expounded in the Lotus Sutra, a major Mahayana scripture, are the supreme manifestation of the Buddha's nature, example, and message.

Buddhism began twenty-five hundred years ago in what is now Nepal. The founder was a man named Siddhartha Gautama. According to a famous traditional biography, Siddhartha left his sleeping wife and infant son behind and sneaked out of his father's palace to join those who practiced meditation, yoga, and ascetic disciplines in order to find a truth that would liberate them from the endless cycle of suffering and rebirth. Siddhartha studied with these wandering holy men, but finding their teachings wanting, he invented his own approach to physical, mental, and spiritual practice. Through his method, which he called the "Middle Way," he attained complete awakening to the liberating truth the holy men sought. This truth brought him freedom from suffering and the causes of suffering, and the gift of teaching others. From that moment, he was called "the Buddha," the Awakened One. For forty-five years, until his death, he taught many disciples.

Nikkyo Niwano had an unusual gift for relating the teachings of the Buddha, a man of another time who was largely a teacher of monks, to the lives of ordinary people in war-torn and rapidly urbanizing Japan. As Kosho says in this book, her grandfather was a man who wholeheartedly wanted to make every person he met happy. He tried to do this not by charming them or entertaining them, not by selling them something, but by helping them see their lives from the Buddha's perspective, which is clearly revealed in the Lotus Sutra, and by showing them how to apply the Buddha's teachings.

He taught individuals, small groups, and large assemblies. He saw everyone and every circumstance that entered his life as valuable and taught others how to see whatever entered their lives that way too. He taught his followers how to use the Buddha's fundamental teachings—the Four Noble Truths, the Eightfold Path, the Six Perfections, the Twelve Causes and Conditions, and the Ten

Suchnesses—not only to understand themselves and others but also to pinpoint how problems could be solved.

Further, together with those basic doctrines, he communicated to them the thought and practice of bodhisattvas who devote themselves to perfect awakening to the universal truth not only for themselves but also for many people. He taught so much more about how to live a truly meaningful life helping liberate others from sufferings than did contemporary Japanese heirs to long-standing Buddhist traditions that ordinary people flocked to study and practice what he taught.

Nikkyo Niwano and his followers created more than two hundred Dharma centers in Japan and other countries, where members gather for religious activities including *hoza,* which are sessions of group interaction based on the Buddha's teachings.

The Buddha's teachings are based on three facts of our experience that can be easily recognized. The first is often called "dependent origination" or "the truth of causation": causes and conditions combine to create effects and rewards. Everything, according to the Buddha, exists because of causes and conditions that make it possible for it to exist. We can see this readily in the case of ordinary things like a kitchen table. The kitchen table exists because someone needed it, someone thought of how to make it, and one or more people made it. It is made of wood because it is made where wood is plentiful; wood exists because of trees; and trees exist because of sunlight, soil, and water. It continues to stay in place in your kitchen because of the law of gravity. It continues to keep its shape because your house protects it from the weather. There are, of course, many more causes and conditions of the existence of the table, and we could trace all of those causes back to further causes. When those causes and conditions change, the table will cease to be.

Causes of the table, like wood, the designer, the carpenter, can be quickly listed; conditions also needed for its continued existence are almost endless, such as the table's continuing to be protected from the weather, not being broken up to use as firewood, and so forth.

To us as heirs to modern biology, chemistry, and physics, "dependent origination" may seem like old news, at least as far as the kitchen table and the visible universe are concerned. But the Buddha took this insight further.

Not only tables depend for their existence on causes and conditions: so do we, and so does our discomfort and suffering. The causes and conditions of suffering are not only in the physical realm but also in the mental, emotional, and moral realms. We live in a stream of cause-and-effect, in which our own thoughts and actions are both causes and effects.

The causes of suffering have a lot to do with what we call "attitudes" and "intentions." The Buddha taught that our desires and our ignorance, that is, our inability to see and accept things as they are, inevitably cause dissatisfaction, anxiety, uneasiness, physical and emotional pain, isolation and alienation, and other forms of suffering. But the good news is that what has a cause can be cured.

We of course have moments of pleasure, joy, and satisfaction; the Buddha did not deny that fact. That brings us to the second fact of our experience that the Buddha taught: the truth of impermanence. Even our moments of joy and satisfaction are tinged with our knowledge of their impermanence. Just as they are, they will not last forever. Often we find ourselves pulled around by desires for things that do not in the end satisfy for very long.

Greed, hatred, and delusion, which the Buddha identified as the big obstacles to a happy life, are closely related to our cycles of desire, satisfaction, and the fading of satisfaction. We want something, and we become greedy about it. Someone denies us something we want or inflicts on us something we don't want, and we hate that person or institution. We fall into the trap of thinking that obtaining everything we want or avoiding what we don't want will make us happy forever, and this always proves to be a false expectation, a delusion.

At all stages of life, things slip away from our grasp, while unwelcome things occur. Things change, people change, we change. Things that depend for their existence on causes and conditions always arise when those causes and conditions arise, and they perish when those causes and conditions cease. The Buddha is famous for his instructions to his disciples on his deathbed: "Do not grieve," he said, "for coming to an end is the fate of all conditioned things." The Buddha thereby reminded his disciples that he himself was a conditioned thing.

The third fact of experience taught by the Buddha is that everything is characterized by not having a permanent, independent self. This is true even of the awakened Buddha. This is felt by modern people to be a controversial proposition, as we are taught to create a self, an identity. Buddhists recognize that creating a self and an identity in the Western sense is fine—necessary, in fact—as long as we realize that these identities of ours are neither eternal nor uncaused. They are caused and conditioned by our personal histories. In fact, they are largely "constructed" from our habitual responses. Even our consciousness, which sometimes feels to us like a self, depends on causes and conditions.

Again, this sounds like bad news but is, in fact, good news. Would you like to be forever the person you were at six? At twelve? At twenty? The fact that you yourself can deepen your insights, change your behavior, improve your character, commit to your marriage, and love people you once hated is due to the power you can find to change causes and conditions, particularly those that you yourself create. Good actions of body, speech, and mind lead to good results for the actor; bad actions likewise lead to bad results for oneself. If we had permanent, uncaused selves, this easily observable fact would not be true.

Why are the Buddha's teachings called "The Light of Asia" and not "The Gloom Report"? This is because the Buddha taught that suffering, depending as it does on causes and conditions, will end if those causes and conditions are seen clearly, understood, and changed. We have the power to greatly reduce our own suffering and the sufferings of others. Suffering is not random. Buddhist teachings applied in daily life empower us because we find that we *can* generate good intentions, compassionate and helpful causes and conditions that produce happiness. With some practice we can in each situation see and accept things as they are. With instruction and practice we can eliminate the specific causes of each moment of suffering and create new causes and conditions that will bring happiness. While desire is very subtle and powerful, and changing our fundamental personality and character is difficult, over time we can become happier if we devote ourselves to happiness-creating actions and repent of ones that caused harm.

As a teacher of Buddhist wisdom and as the president-designate of Rissho Kosei-kai, Kosho Niwano devotes herself to studying and practicing the Buddha's teachings, particularly those found in the Buddha's early sutras and the Lotus Sutra. She has also taken on a special task, one that has resulted in this book. She has worked at penetrating deeply into and clarifying for herself and others the essence of her grandfather's teaching and practice as expressed in his words and deeds and illuminated by the expressions of his radiant personality.

In this her first book, she focuses on the essence of her grandfather's understanding of the Lotus Sutra. She identifies two themes—she compares them to the two lenses of a pair of glasses—through which she can express both concisely and profoundly the essence of her grandfather's religious attainment and teaching: "the Eternal Original Buddha's vow" and "revealing buddha-nature."

Buddha-nature is the Buddha in everyone's heart, our own potential for wisdom and a deep compassionate desire to help others. The Eternal Original Buddha's vow is the profound and long-lasting intention of the Eternal Original Buddha. This Buddha has existed from the infinite past and appears in many forms throughout the ages to guide and succor all living beings through the teaching of the Dharma. The Eternal Original Buddha always wishes to devote himself energetically and completely to bringing everyone out of suffering. Not only that, he desires to bring us all into a freedom, compassion, and wisdom exactly like his own.

Kosho Niwano writes about her grandfather in this book, quoting him in every chapter. But what she expresses is also her own deep understanding, nurtured in a living Buddhist faith and practice. She owes this understanding both to her grandfather and to her own practice and realization. Like her grandfather, she wholeheartedly wants every one of us to be happy. She tells stories about her grandfather and others to help us grasp the truths Shakyamuni Buddha discovered, truths that can be seen and practiced in our daily lives. For example, she writes:

> The theory of causes leading to effects notes that good causes lead to good effects and bad causes lead to bad effects. The founder always focused on the way that good causes lead to good effects. Having encountered the Lotus Sutra, he took an extra step, based on basic Buddhist teaching, and chose to see such good causes and good effects and to recognize the people one meets every day as good causes or good

conditions. That is how the theory of causes leading to effects should be applied with the wisdom of the Lotus Sutra. This is the view of dependent origination taught in the sutra as capable of liberating everyone 100 percent.

This is not just another book about how to be spiritual. It is in its own way a systematic and comprehensive presentation of what the Buddhist life is and how to live it, through the eyes of one devoted to making it fully understandable to us. It shares both practical guidance and deep philosophy. It is a book for everyone who is ready to consider walking the Buddha's path wholeheartedly. And it achieves the most elusive of all goals of writing: it can be understood, appreciated, and loved by all.

Dr. Miriam Levering
Professor Emerita
University of Tennessee

# PREFACE

As a grandchild of Founder Nikkyo Niwano and also as an individual seeker, I want to accurately pass along the teachings that the founder embodied throughout his lifetime and share them with as many people as possible. It is with this purpose that I have undertaken to write this book.

To that end, I started on two things. The first was to revisit the huge number of Dharma talks and writings by the founder. The second was to speak with persons both within and outside our organization who had had a connection with the founder and to listen to their suggestions.

These two efforts constitute the challenge of getting to the essence of the "picture of the founder" that remains even today in the minds of the many people who have been liberated by his teachings, and they became a unique opportunity to draw near to an understanding of the founder's achievement.

Founder Niwano's deep human empathy and passion remained unchanged throughout his life after he encountered the true spirit of the Lotus Sutra, "to liberate 100 percent of all people," and comprehended the One Dharma as the key with a perfect fit. Among the huge number of Dharma talks by Founder Niwano, I felt he certainly must have left us the treasures we need to move forward in the direction of the Place of Jewels, the stage of Mahayana nirvana. All I needed was the capacity to recognize them.

No sooner had my writing started, however, than it seemed at times that I was adrift in a sea of the founder's various Dharma talks as I sought to find the deep inner source from which they all sprang, even though as his granddaughter I had been privileged to live with him. It became apparent that the teachings of Founder Niwano, who always did his best in every encounter to bring happiness to people and peace to the world, could be considered too extensive to encapsulate easily.

After trial and error, I decided to return once again to the Founder Niwano who lives in my heart. Using his Dharma talks as the basis, I gave considerable thought to such points as what sort of person Founder Niwano actually was, why he said the things that he did, and how those words affected the situations and the thinking of the people around him. Further, I also decided to progress in my writing by taking examples of how members and senior leaders guided others to liberation while at the same time achieving it themselves.

If we could fully comprehend Founder Niwano's faith in the Lotus Sutra and appreciate the One Dharma that he was able to grasp, our lives would surely be enriched. So I thought we needed something like special glasses that any of us could put on at any time, wherever we happened to be.

I fitted those glasses with two lenses, one called "the Eternal Original Buddha's vow" and the other called "revealing the buddha-nature." That enabled the realm of the One Dharma lying deep within the Innumerable Meanings—the source of the founder's many teachings and individual guidance—to gradually rise to the surface, almost like a 3-D image.

What I could then see was the answer I sought, "to put one's hands together in prayer, shining a light on the buddha-nature of all people, and discovering the workings of the Buddha in our midst at the present time." Once I realized this, I was filled with a profound peace of mind and sense of hope, as if I were facing the warmth of a brilliant light spilling out from the end of a limitless tunnel.

Of course, I have a lot left to learn, and I do not presume to think I have succeeded in conveying the full impact of the greatness of Founder Niwano's personality. But I have demonstrated here the process of striving to follow in his footsteps, seeking the world of light that he sought, so as to achieve my wish of eventually inheriting that light and passing it along to the future.

It is my heartfelt wish that each and every one of you will receive the light that is the spirit of the Lotus Sutra, and that all of you will lead spiritually rich and satisfying lives.

Kosho Niwano
President-designate
Rissho Kosei-kai

# 1 Discovering the Light
## *Enlightenment*

When our hearts are constantly filled with the joy of faith achieved by the teachings of the Buddha, the world we live in transforms into an exquisitely enjoyable place. Beauty is everywhere we look, and everyone we meet seems a bodhisattva.

—*Niwano Nikkyo Howa Senshu*
(Selected Dharma Talks of Nikkyo Niwano)

It was on the morning of December 8, just as the morning star appeared in the sky, when the Bodhisattva's mind was as clear as the breaking day, that he at last attained perfect enlightenment. From that time on, his ability to look at all things was different from that of ordinary people. He was able to perceive clearly the ultimate reality of all things, unhindered by superficial phenomena: he had gained the eyes of a buddha.

Upon attaining enlightenment, he said, "Wonderful! Wonderful! All living beings possess the wisdom and the virtuous sign of the Tathagata [the highest epithet of a buddha], but they do not realize this because of their attachment to desires and illusions.

When Shakyamuni looked on the world through the eyes of a buddha, he noticed that everything appeared completely changed. Animals, plants, and human beings all seemed bathed in such glory and brilliance that it was as if they were pervaded by the same life as the Buddha. His spontaneous "Wonderful! Wonderful!" was uttered out of his great joy at discovering the ultimate reality of all things.

Founder Nikkyo Niwano wrote about the moment when Shakyamuni attained perfect enlightenment in his book *Shakyamuni Buddha: A Narrative Biography.*

It is said that in the moment Shakyamuni (referred to as "the Bodhisattva" at the start of the above quotation) attained buddhahood and perfect wisdom, everything in his sight appeared to be shining with light. Perhaps that is one reason that we speak of attaining buddhahood as "becoming enlightened," including the sense of seeing everything as shining with light.

What the founder is telling us here is that when we can detect the essence of what is shining in the people we meet, when we have the eyes to see the light in things that are inherently shining, this means that we are attaining buddhahood.

What kind of place do we see when we look at our world with this kind of sight? We see a world where all things are precious and all people appear as buddhas. No matter what we encounter, we do not flinch, believing that everything occurs so as to lead us toward self-realization, and we can live at peace there.

The world is essentially a beautiful, radiant place, but since the lenses of our minds are covered with dirt, it seems to us unclean. If we scrub the dirt from our minds, the world as it is immediately becomes the Land of Tranquil Light. This idea is at the very heart of the teachings of the Lotus Sutra. (*Shinshaku Hokke Sambu-kyo* [New Commentary on the Threefold Lotus Sutra], vol. 2, p. 85)

## 2 Living with the Power That Gives Us Life
### *Dependent Origination*

We must awaken to the principle of causation in such a way that we get a deep, gut feeling for it. Without understanding its truth, we cannot say we have really been liberated [freed from suffering].
—*Niwano Nikkyo Howa Senshu*
(Selected Dharma Talks of Nikkyo Niwano)

Founder Nikkyo Niwano has said, "The Lotus Sutra is all about awakening to causes and conditions" and "Buddhism does not shed its light on those without a true understanding of causes and conditions." What constitutes an understanding of causation and of causes and conditions, and moreover an understanding that causes Buddhism to shed its light?

One day, the founder was attending a ceremony to commemorate the anniversary of a Rissho Kosei-kai Dharma center. A member of the young women's group was attempting to serve tea in the anteroom where the founder and others were waiting for the ceremony to begin. Perhaps because she felt nervous, since she was unaccustomed to wearing a kimono, the young woman spilled the tea on the table.

Those present caught their collective breath, but the founder's face lit up as he said, "Well, look at that! The tea is spreading all over the table into what looks like an auspicious pattern. This is a sign that today's events will help spread the teaching even further. The Buddha is smiling. This is great, something for which we should all be grateful!"

The tension eased, and everybody was relieved to hear these words. They were also grateful for the feeling that they could now get on with their happy day with a renewed sense of cohesion. The atmosphere was suddenly warmer and calmer as everyone appreciated seeing the founder's solicitude for the young woman's feelings, and how his outlook and spirit led him to use every opportunity to discover the joy even in something that might be viewed as a failure.

When you look with unfettered eyes, change becomes very apparent. To gracefully adapt to change is the right way to live. (*Shinshaku Hokke Sambu-kyo* [New Commentary on the Threefold Lotus Sutra], vol. 7, p. 101)

How could the founder immediately find in such a sudden occurrence just the right thing to say to make everyone happy? I do not think we can simply say that this showed his personality. It was because his whole life revolved around the wish of the Buddha, who helps everyone possessed of karmic conditions or connections with him to awaken to the Truth and make the fullest use of his or her life.

Through karmic connections we can learn of the Buddha's wish that all people make the best use of their strengths and potential for good. Karmic connections are everything that happens around us and every person that we meet. The founder always saw the people he was with through the eyes of compassion and tried to make them happy and realize the Buddha's wish through the influence of wisdom, which maximizes the potential of all karmic connections. The warmth of his personality illuminated everything around him.

How can we perceive karmic connections so that we, too, can have wisdom and compassion like the founder's?

As we can see in the expression "good causes lead to good results and bad causes lead to bad results," people are affected by what they have done. Looking at this expression from the perspective of the Buddha, it means that the color of your spirit becomes manifest. If you can change the color of your spirit, you can become a being with a brilliant aura like the Buddha's and attain a state in which you lose all anxiety and gain peace of mind. As Shakyamuni said, "Differences there are none; I and all living beings are equal." (Speech at Fumon Hall, Tokyo, September 23, 1973)

Even when we are aware of the need to act, it is not so easy for us to change ourselves or reform our behavior. Sometimes we find that no matter how hard we try, we come up against things that we cannot change. What can we do in a situation like this?

A member of Rissho Kosei-kai was the mother of two sons. The elder son required kidney dialysis to stay alive. The other son apparently had a girlfriend but made no attempt to introduce her to his family as a way of demonstrating his intention to marry her.

"I just want to be happy, and in the hope of becoming happy, I embraced the faith and have played a role in our Dharma center," the mother said. "But my elder son's health does not improve, and my younger son still has not introduced us to his girlfriend. How did we become such a dysfunctional family? How long do I have to keep on with my religious practice before my family is liberated?"

These were the concerns that the mother revealed during a *hoza,* or Dharma circle, session (a unique form of group interaction that is guided by experienced leaders). In reply, she was told the following by the leader.

"In former ages, your son's illness would have been incurable. Thanks to the advances of modern medicine, he is still alive. Your younger son probably does not bring his girlfriend around because he thinks it might upset his brother. He must actually be a kind boy. You must be a successful mother to have raised such good children. You should be pleased with your family."

Hearing this, the mother accepted her current situation. Tears welled up in her eyes, and her heart was filled with warmth. That same evening, she wrote to her sons describing her newfound feelings.

The next day, both sons thanked her for her letter, telling her that it really pleased them, and this made her deeply happy.

"The gift of having been born," "being given life"—if you truly understand these things, your buddha-nature can be properly revealed, and you can live a responsible life without falsehood. (*Hosshin* [Raising Aspirations], July 1990, p. 16)

What was that warm feeling that the mother experienced?

Her elder son would probably continue to need dialysis. She could not tell whether her younger son would introduce his girlfriend to the family or not. But because of the karmic connections between her and her sons, she had also been given new life as a mother, and her desire for their happiness had given her the will to try to overcome her difficulties up to that point. By supporting one another they were sustained in their lives.

When you have the perception that present "karmic connections" are why you are living and being given life, then you are living in the world of dependent origination, a teaching that moved the founder deeply. This is the approach of the Lotus Sutra. When you achieve an understanding of causes and conditions in this way, that will be when the teaching of the Buddha begins to emit its light.

> If the teachings of Buddhism are boiled down, we can say they are what gives us an understanding of the true reality: that we are sustained by all things in heaven and on earth and that we are caused to live by things that are invisible to us. (*Yakushin* [Progress], April 1979, pp. 13–14)

## 3  One Hundred Percent Liberation
### *The Lotus Sutra*

The Lotus Sutra does not work in a specific way like a particular drug can cure a particular disease or a certain treatment cure a certain condition. Rather, it is like a drug that cures all illnesses by eliminating them at the root or a fundamental treatment that can make every single person completely healthy.

—*Shinshaku Hokke Sambu-kyo*
(New Commentary on the Threefold Lotus Sutra)

When Founder Nikkyo Niwano encountered the Lotus Sutra, he was greatly moved and declared, "The Lotus Sutra is the teaching that can bring liberation to all people, 100 percent!" He thought so because he had a genuine feeling that the Lotus Sutra is composed in such a way that every person who reads it with an open mind and a straightforward attitude will be liberated (freed from suffering).

So, what does it mean to read the Lotus Sutra with an open mind and a straightforward attitude? How should we study and apply the Lotus Sutra so that we will all be liberated, 100 percent?

What does it mean to be liberated? In any event, liberation does not mean that our problems will all disappear if we undergo religious training or that we will get what we want if we are diligent in our religious practice.

> When I heard Rev. Sukenobu Arai* explain that from one meaning (the universal Truth) arise a million meanings, which can again be condensed into one, for the first time I was awakened to the following. Until then I had pursued my studies in piecemeal fashion, but when I heard this truth presented in a nutshell, for example, as it is in chapter 2 of the Sutra of Innumerable Meanings ("Preaching"), which says that "Innumerable Meanings arise from the One Dharma," I could comprehend that all things are means to make the buddha-nature manifest. My joy at that moment was beyond description. (*Kono Michi* [The Path That We Have Walked], p. 38)

The teaching of dependent origination is the foundation of Buddhism. This teaching says that everything in the world exists as a result of the meeting between causes and conditions. No matter what happens, if you look squarely at an event, search out the reasons it occurred and transcend them, you can distance yourself from suffering. In other words, it teaches, "To attain happiness, do no evil but play a good leading role at certain times and a good supporting role at other times."

However, will all people really be able to change their behavior as soon as they receive this teaching? The reality is that we cannot

---

* Rev. Arai was a scholar of Chinese and Buddhist classics who lectured about the Lotus Sutra to the founder before Rissho Kosei-kai was established.

always change our basic attitudes or behavior even when we would like to. If we admit that this is true, it seems to lead to the conclusion that only a handful of particularly strong-willed people can be happy. That would preclude "100 percent liberation."

The founder had this to say: "When he achieved his awakening under the Bodhi tree, Shakyamuni also realized that the world exists through the principle of causes and conditions. As he later expounded the Lotus Sutra, however, he came to realize the state of true awakening in relation to the solving of problems that arise from causes and conditions. That is why understanding the Lotus Sutra means understanding everything."

As we can see from this statement, it is essential for us to assume as our own the true standpoint of the Lotus Sutra, which is capable of liberating everyone 100 percent.

> *Shravakas,* disciples who hear and follow the Buddha's teaching, and *pratyekabuddhas,* those engaged in religious training without a teacher, are beings who have sought their own complete self-realization or emancipation from the sufferings of life. It is truly commendable for anyone to have such a goal and work to achieve it. I wonder, however, if all people on earth can actually achieve such a state of mind. If we look at this as a practical problem, we are forced to say that such an achievement is close to impossible. (*Shinshaku Hokke Sambu-kyo* [New Commentary on the Threefold Lotus Sutra], vol. 8, p. 24)

The theory of causes leading to effects notes that good causes lead to good effects and bad causes lead to bad effects. The founder always focused on the way that good causes lead to good effects. Having encountered the Lotus Sutra, he took an extra step, based on basic Buddhist teaching, and chose to see such good causes and good effects and to recognize the people one meets every day as good causes or good conditions. That is how the theory of causes leading to effects should be applied with the wisdom of the Lotus Sutra. This is the view of dependent origination taught in the sutra as capable of liberating everyone 100 percent.

> The "Universal and Great Wisdom" allows us to realize the ultimate reality of all things and is the wisdom that allows us to see that all people and all living things are equally capable of attaining buddhahood. The Lotus Sutra is based on this Universal and Great Wisdom and is, in fact, the doctrine expounding it. (*Shinshaku Hokke Sambu-kyo* [New Commentary on the Threefold Lotus Sutra], vol. 5, p. 299)

When we attain a state of mind in which we can see every encounter as a cause of happiness, that is what is meant by "the Lotus Sutra liberating every person, 100 percent." The belief that every person exists in order to achieve happiness is the approach taken by the Lotus Sutra. When we embrace this approach, we become aware of happiness and can acquire true joy. This is precisely how we are liberated by the teachings of the Lotus Sutra.

When we believe that the conditions we encounter are always leading us along the path to happiness, we have taken the first step to liberation. All we need to do after that is to confirm this through the events of our everyday lives. It is not true that a person cannot be liberated without religious faith. Actually we are all liberated, although many people are not yet aware of this. The process of liberation is certain. Thus the important thing is to accustom yourself to always seeing that all things you encounter can be causes of happiness.

The founder was a person who strongly believed this.

True Buddhist enlightenment is to believe from the bottom of your heart that "all living things are endowed with the buddha-nature." Everything starts from there. (*Niwano Nikkyo Howa Senshu* [Selected Dharma Talks of Nikkyo Niwano], special volume, p. 64)

Awareness especially arises through contact with other people. A certain husband and wife happened to both break an arm on the same day. The husband could not go to his work, nor could the wife do her housework or her duties at her Dharma center. She was discouraged, but a leader of the center said to her, "Both of you having a broken arm will at least mean that you can understand the pain and frustration the other is feeling and sympathize with each other. This is an opportunity for heart-to-heart communication. I think this will help you to be a really happy couple."

The wife had been upset and unhappy, thinking only about why such an unpleasant thing had happened to them, and was unable even to talk about the situation. But when the Dharma center leader pointed out the opportunity for heart-to-heart communication and she was able to look at things that way, she experienced warm feelings of happiness.

When something bad happens to us, we suffer by tending to become obsessed with what occurred and think we will be happy as soon as we solve the problem. However, even if a solution is achieved, that is not 100 percent liberation. When we take solving our problems as our goal, we can just make things more difficult.

When we look at the true nature of human beings from a standpoint that is enlightened to the ultimate reality of all things, because that nature is after all the buddha-nature, we can see that all teachings ultimately come back to the one point of becoming aware of the buddha-nature within us, becoming aware of it in all other people, and helping them to become aware of it and develop it. (*Shinshaku Hokke Sambu-kyo* [New Commentary on the Threefold Lotus Sutra], vol. 5, p. 302)

All phenomena and events occur in order for us to find happiness and are gifts of the Buddha that appear in accordance with what is necessary. When we try out this belief, we can find in all the encounters of everyday life the Buddha's wish to help us make the best of ourselves and achieve true happiness.

We then begin to make the effort to focus our minds on discovering how the Buddha helps us to make the best of ourselves. When we understand this and become aware that we are living in the midst of liberation, a joyous world evolves toward realization.

The world of the Lotus Sutra is a joyful world. According to how you discover that joy and see things as the workings of the Buddha, the world of liberation will evolve toward realization for you beyond any confines of time and space. Wouldn't you like to experience such a world?

Liberation arises when we become fully conscious of the Eternal Original Buddha, who is with us at all times. When we are awakened from deep in our being to the fact that we are sustained by the Buddha, we attain true liberation. This is because when we have that unshakable awareness, we can for the first time achieve true contentment that arises from deep in our being. At the same time, everything we say and do begins to be naturally in accord with the Buddha's heart, that is, with the Truth. (*Shinshaku Hokke Sambu-kyo* [New Commentary on the Threefold Lotus Sutra], vol. 9, p. 11)

# 4   Seeing Things as They Are
## *Recognizing the Ultimate Reality*

The Buddha's wisdom is the wisdom that sees things as they really are. When I speak of seeing things as they really are, I mean seeing the essence of things, undistracted by what changes, shifts, or varies. That is, seeing the ultimate reality of all things and correctly perceiving them as whole entities, without taking a biased or one-sided view.

—*San Reizan Meiso* (Meditations from Three Holy Mountains)

Founder Nikkyo Niwano was fond of saying "Things are all right just the way they are." By this he did not mean "Accept your present situation even if it makes you suffer" or "Do nothing, just leave things the way they are." What he meant was, "The people around you and the events you experience will certainly reveal the working of the Buddha if you see them with the eyes of the Buddha's wisdom."

> In the Buddha's eyes, there is no world in the ten directions that is not the Land of Tranquil Light. But because we see

these worlds through the eyes of ignorance, they appear to be filled with delusion and uncleanness. Changing this world into the Land of Tranquil Light necessitates changing the way we human beings see and think about things. (*Shinshaku Hokke Sambu-kyo* [New Commentary on the Threefold Lotus Sutra], vol. 5, pp. 313–14)

Every person has his or her own set of personal values. Thus there is an infinite variety in the way that phenomena are perceived and understood. Such values are almost always based on perceptions of good and bad, profit and loss, personal circumstances, likes and dislikes, or other elements of common sense or personal ways of thinking.

What happens, however, when we view the world, in the founder's words, with the eyes of the Buddha's wisdom?

We should make use of our defilements or desires in a positive way, rather than being obsessed with escaping from them, so that we can bring a lively energy to our world and create harmony in it. That is the wisdom of the Buddha. (*Niwano Nikkyo Howa Senshu* [Selected Dharma Talks of Nikkyo Niwano], special volume, p. 86)

Once there was a young mother who always strove to attain her ideal of being a good daughter-in-law, a good wife, and a good mother. The baby boy she had been blessed with was sickly, however, and whenever she was having a particularly difficult time, the baby's health became worse.

"I am trying so hard every day, why is this happening to me? What will people say about me?" Such thoughts constantly clouded her mind. More than anything else, however, she worried about how long her son would be able to live, and was always uneasy.

Her worries were at their peak when the baby would begin to run a high fever again. All of this made her wonder if she needed to reflect on her lack of sufficient gratitude to her parents. She had always acted with the sincere intention of being as dutiful as possible to her parents, however, and could not think of how she might have disappointed them. With no improvement in her satisfaction in sight and full of worry, she approached the founder, asking, "What can I do to keep my baby son from running these fevers?"

At this the founder said, "Let's see—let me hold your baby for a minute."

He took the infant in his arms and held him for a while. Gently stroking the baby's head, he said, "Well, well, you're a good little boy. So this is how you're bringing up Mommy." To the young mother he added, "I think you now realize how much you are indebted to your parents for raising you." And that was all.

Those who make the effort to put into practice their faith in the Eternal Original Buddha become able to see the Eternal Original Buddha and hear his teaching in everything they perceive and everything they experience. (*Niwano Nikkyo Howa Senshu* [Selected Dharma Talks of Nikkyo Niwano], special volume, p. 51)

The ultimate reality of all things means that in their form as they are, all things demonstrate their maximum abilities at the present time. (*Kosei,* August 1953, p. 9)

The mother had come to the founder determined to accept any degree of stern advice if it meant finding a way to make her baby well, and she felt somewhat let down by the founder's mild response. Even so, she found herself thinking, "So that is it. That is what parents have to do. We have to experience all sorts of difficulties to raise our children." Merely coming to this realization, however, did not bring down her infant son's fever. She still had to rush the child to the hospital on frequent occasions.

> If all human beings are able to see things as they really are, with the eye of the perfect wisdom of the Buddha, this world will become the Land of Tranquil Light here and now. (*Shinshaku Hokke Sambu-kyo* [New Commentary on the Threefold Lotus Sutra], vol. 5, p. 314)

In the course of these repeated alarms, however, something gradually dawned on her.

"If my child's time has come, it will come even if the doctor is right there. So let me do my best to help my baby regain his health with love and tender care now while I can. Let me live each day the way the Buddha would want me to do. That will be enough. It is all that I can do."

We often consider faith as something that will free us from our difficulties and torments. We start out assuming that such suffering should not exist. Most things usually do not work out exactly as we would like, so we think, "This is not the way I wanted this to be. I wanted it to be like this." The result is more suffering. But the founder taught us that suffering is a message from the Buddha, so we should gain realization from it.

> The Buddha eye refers to the way of viewing things comprehensively, synthesizing all other ways of seeing things. The Buddha eye not only sees clearly the ultimate reality of all things in the universe but also watches over them all with compassion. (*Shinshaku Hokke Sambu-kyo* [New Commentary on the Threefold Lotus Sutra], vol. 4, p. 40)

The wisdom of the Buddha is wisdom that sees things as they really are. And it is wisdom that makes the best of things as they really are. If we can discover the working of the Buddha's compassion not only in the midst of good times but also in the midst of painful events, then the present moment will always be meaningful and valuable to us. I cannot help but feel very strongly that this is the secret of where true happiness lies.

It might be difficult to discover the working of the Buddha in every situation. If, however, you accustom yourself to raising your heart's antenna to pick up that signal and continually do your best to feel joy in every moment, your wisdom will be enriched and strengthened. To develop the wisdom to make the most of each present moment is the reason that we are living.

The most important thing is "eyes that can see." In today's world, Japan has the potential to become heaven as well as the potential to turn into hell. I think we can say that which occurs, which will develop, depends on the point of view we take. The bodhisattva Kannon is said to be the "Regarder of the Cries of the World." When the bodhisattva "regards" the world, it is with vision that can see the heart, right through to the ultimate reality. As we strive to see the ultimate reality of this world, I think that we will find that the key to making this world a pure and heavenly land lies hidden in that very act of striving. (*Yakushin* [Progress], January 1978, p. 13)

## 5 Finding Happiness in Our Present Situation
### *Religious Merit*

The Lotus Sutra is full of merit. Wherever you read in it you will find only merit. Thus, when you read it with care and put it into practice with an open mind, you can hardly avoid gaining merit.

—*Niwano Nikkyo Howa Senshu*
(Selected Dharma Talks of Nikkyo Niwano)

"Don't worry. Everything happens the way the Buddha intends." To what extent have these words of Founder Nikkyo Niwano helped me out, even to this day?

Soon after my son was born, a type of eczema developed on his face. Normally he was a good-tempered baby, but when he was sleepy he tended to cry; his temperature then rose and made his face itch so badly that he could not sleep.

To keep him from scratching the rash and to help him get even a little sleep, I would sit on the sofa every night and hold him on my lap until morning.

This went on for several months, and though we tried everything, the rash not only failed to improve but spread all over his

face. After four months, the only unaffected area was the tip of
his nose. When I was alone with my son in my arms, looking at
his little face and wondering how long this condition would continue, I would pity him and feel so sorry for him that I wept.

Then one day an idea occurred to me.

"If my son did not have this rash, what would our lives be like
now? Since he is our fourth child, I would probably feel safe leaving him at home with other family members and go out to tend
to my other duties. He would probably grow up without having
been held in his mother's arms very often."

> It would hardly be possible for our minds to change and our
> lives not to change as well. Our lives must change. Our state
> of mind changes because of our faith, and with this change
> in our thinking comes a change in life. These are the mer-
> its of religious practice. Therefore, there is always merit in
> faith. (*Shinshaku Hokke Sambu-kyo* [New Commentary on
> the Threefold Lotus Sutra], vol. 7, p. 173)

Looking at my situation in this way, the time I was spending
holding my son began to appear as a precious gift from the Buddha to us both.

It also dawned on me that despite his face's being afflicted
with the bright red eczema, his three sisters were always gathering
around to hold and dandle him, exclaiming how cute he was.

My husband and parents were also doing their best to support
us, telling me "Don't worry, he will soon recover" or "He looks a
little better today, don't you think?"

Thinking about the love they showed warmed my spirit, and I
began to feel really happy.

If I had only been concerning myself about what I may have
been doing wrong or what else I could do to help make my son

get better, I would probably not have noticed the affection being offered by everyone in the family, and I would never have experienced the happiness that I felt then.

The founder always said, "Happiness is never achieved by running around looking for it; it is something you discover and become aware of in the here and now."

Instead of denying the existence of a problem or becoming obsessed with trying to solve it, learning to find the joy that exists in a situation as it is opens for us the true way to liberation. In fact, if you are able to find the joy in things the way they are, you can actually feel happy to encounter a problem. In other words, just by acquiring this way of looking at things, your life will evolve in a rich and meaningful way that corresponds to it.

I felt the words of the founder coming back to me: "Everything happens the way the Buddha intends." If we truly believe this, if we are sure of it from the bottom of our hearts, the degree of happiness we can find in life will become immense. When we discover the working of the Buddha in every phenomenon, even worry and distress can be transformed into merit for us all.

In my case, as the days went by, I suddenly realized that my son's eczema had finally subsided to the point where it did not really bother him anymore.

In most cases, the usual, uneventful state of affairs is one of merit. People with true faith are the ones who can sense this. (*Niwano Nikkyo Howa Senshu* [Selected Dharma Talks of Nikkyo Niwano], special volume, p. 119)

When we recover from an illness or maintain good health, we are enjoying great merit. It is in the here and now, however, in our present situation that our true riches lie.

## 6 Making the Best Use of Everything
*Awareness of Our Value*
*in Having Been Given Life*

One thing I greatly value in the Lotus Sutra is its logic of making the best of every opportunity.

—*Hosshin* (Raising Aspirations), July 1990

Founder Nikkyo Niwano used to meet difficult problems head-on and with verve, saying, "Now things are becoming interesting."

When something unpleasant happens or we are suffering irksome interpersonal relations, we are quick to think, "Did I do something wrong? Why do I have to go through this?" We do this even though we are supposed to be aware that all things happen through the divine arrangements of the Buddha for the purpose of giving us happiness in life.

Of course, everything always happens for a reason. However, the viewpoint of the Buddha toward problems differs from our own viewpoint. That is, the way the Buddha sees things appears to be only slightly different from the way we see them, but that slight difference makes all the difference in the way the world is perceived and evolves.

This is what Shakyamuni called a good friend: he said that someone who is your exact opposite is your good friend, in fact, your best friend. That is the approach, and it is one that changes your thinking. The source of this teaching is the Lotus Sutra. (*Niwano Nikkyo Howa Senshu* [Selected Dharma Talks of Nikkyo Niwano], vol. 4, p. 146)

When something unpleasant happens or you meet someone you do not like, it is important to think about the reasons for your unhappiness or dislike, reflect on causes that may be within yourself, and try to change them. This process takes time, however, and it seldom imparts immediate joy or energy for living.

When you see people in this world as being good or bad, nothing ever seems to please you, and nothing ever seems to be helpful to you. However, an attitude that regards every person as an ally and is prepared to live and let live is the attitude of the Buddha. Whether they are good or evil, everyone must eventually find happiness. In this concept lies the greatness of the Lotus Sutra. (*Niwano Nikkyo Howa Senshu* [Selected Dharma Talks of Nikkyo Niwano], vol. 4, p. 146)

There once was a man who had agreed to be the guarantor for the loan of a friend. It became apparent, however, that his friend could not repay the loan, and so he found himself saddled with the debt.

He realized he did have a legal responsibility in the matter and went to apologize and ask for more time, but he really had no idea what to do about the situation; he was distraught.

Everything turned around 180 degrees thanks to a comment from the founder, who said, "You have been given the opportunity to do something good. You should be grateful for the chance to gain merit. Even if it is for something like a debt, the act of humbling yourself to others is one of respecting others and revering their buddha-nature and thus constitutes bodhisattva practice. So you can feel at ease and consider dealing with the debt as a way for you to attain buddhahood."

The man realized that what he considered as only a humiliation was a way of progressing on the Buddha Way and completely changed his attitude—he had discovered value in the very act of humbling himself. With this, something he had considered as an onerous duty was transformed into something he was pleased to do for the sake of attaining buddhahood.

To humble oneself as a kind of religious training to make up for a customary lack of humility somehow misses the real point, however.

From the Buddha's viewpoint of making the best use of every opportunity, problems occur in order to lead us to fulfill the goal of performing bodhisattva practice. From the viewpoint of the Buddha's world, rather than seek the reason that problems occur, we should look for their purpose.

> When we become aware of the worth of our being alive and being given life, we should not shortchange ourselves but live our lives for all they are worth. (*San Reizan Meiso* [Meditations from Three Holy Mountains], p. 23)

If only we can recognize the true worth of what is happening right now, even problems we have been considering as painful will change into issues we need to deal with in order to attain happiness and are thus occurring through the arrangements of the Buddha.

We have been born in order to achieve joy. We came into this world holding the ticket to happiness—our buddha-nature. We have the same spirit as the Buddha; all we need to do is become aware of it, make it manifest, and share that warmhearted spirit with each other. This is why in life we meet various people and why various things happen to us.

When we become aware of our value in having been given life here and now, we can discover true happiness and become able to experience it. This empowers us to live full and forward-looking lives.

# 7   Opening the Heart
## *The First Step toward Buddha-Knowledge*

The buddhas appear in the world only for the one very great purpose of causing all living beings to attain the Buddha-knowledge; in other words, for the sake of causing living beings to obtain enlightenment, realizing that they can become buddhas.

*—Buddhism for Today*

Founder Nikkyo Niwano said that the buddhas appear in the world for a single great cause—to open up the Buddha Way and lead all beings to it so they may become buddhas. For this to happen, our hearts must first of all be open.

When we listen to other people describing their troubles, it is sometimes easier for us to recognize the cause of their problems before we actually hear what they are feeling in their hearts. When this happens, we want to immediately address the cause of their problems and give them useful advice based on our own experiences, asking them, "Why don't you try this?" or "Why don't you do . . . ?"

Our intention may be to help the other person, and our advice may be the right thing to do in terms of common sense. However, no matter how correct the advice, and however appropriate the suggested changes may be, bringing out such suggestions first and foremost will not open up the hearts of other people. They are suffering because they cannot make those changes even though, in fact, they may be aware of the need for them.

Their problems may be ones you have heard about before, something either common to all periods or particular to modern society. For an afflicted person, however, no matter how common a problem may be, it is a serious matter.

Even though the problem may seem familiar, its background and development will be different for every person. The question is whether you can feel truly empathetic toward the individual afflicted with a particular problem. The point is whether in a given opportunity you can interact with the person in the most appropriate way.

The way to get other people to open their hearts is to empathize with whatever they are feeling. Just when they feel you have truly understood and accepted what they have been saying, that is when their hearts have been opened. In this state, they become willing to accept what you say to them.

> When we speak of revealing the buddha-nature, we are not talking about something unattainable. . . . When you see a sick child and move to help, when you see someone in trouble and feel as if his or her problems were your own . . . such things come quite naturally, but they are nothing but the buddha-nature revealing itself. (*Kosei,* October 1976, pp. 14–15)

The Buddha teaches us to reveal our buddha-nature and become buddhas and to discover the buddha-nature in the people we meet, recognize it, and revere it. When we do this, they also become able to recognize their buddha-nature, awaken to their own value, and move naturally onto the Buddha Way.

When I was in junior high school, my mother became unwell and was admitted to a hospital, probably as a result of accumulated fatigue. Even after she came home, she continued to have to rest in bed. Many people were worried about her and tried to help by giving her advice, telling her what she had done wrong and offering encouraging words. My mother was impatient, thinking she had to hurry and get better, but her body did not respond, and she failed to recover as quickly as she would have liked.

One evening during this time, the founder was especially concerned about how my mother, his daughter-in-law, was doing; he did not merely inquire but went upstairs to see her in her room. He simply sat down beside her bed and repeated, "You have done a good job, a very good job," all the while rubbing her back.

My mother told us later that at this moment she felt truly that she would like to be a gentle person who could comfort others with kind words when they were suffering, as the founder had done for her.

> Unless you can palpably feel and understand the suffering, worry, and joy of others, you will not be able to explain the Dharma in a way that will be best for them. (*Kosei,* September 1964, p. 11)

The most important thing is to have the ability to understand what other people are experiencing internally, their joys and sorrows.

One time, at a training workshop for members of Rissho Kosei-kai men's groups, someone posed a question to the founder: "It has been ten years since I was posted to my present location. It is not that I feel I am in a rut there, but I do feel ready to test myself somewhere else. Every year during personnel transfer season, I keep thinking that this year I will finally be transferred, but my name never comes up. Please tell me how I should deal with this."

The founder smiled and answered by saying, "Well, you're a lucky fellow! If you think of yourself as putting down roots in that one place and apply yourself thoroughly to your work, you can be blessed with the merit you have accumulated there. Perhaps you can make up your mind to this if you imagine that you are going to live the rest of your life and be buried there."

At this, another man raised his hand to ask a question. "I am now starting my second year at my present job. Until now, for some reason I have been transferred here and there about every two or three years. As soon as I feel I am really getting settled and making a real start in my work, I receive another transfer notice. How am I to deal with this?"

The founder smiled and answered by saying, "Well, you're a lucky fellow, too. Precisely because you do not know when you may be transferred, you can try to do the work of the greatest substance every day so you can move on without regrets. I hope you will throw yourself into your work every day so that when transfer season comes around, you can feel ready to go at any time."

These two pieces of advice, when looked at out of context, seem to contradict each other. In reality, however, they are based on deep understanding and sympathy for what was troubling each individual's mind and were spoken with wisdom rooted in the hope of leading each of the men along the path to happiness and the world of the Buddha. Hearing this story, I could not help but sense the profoundly compassionate nature of the founder's spirit.

The first thing to remember is to rid yourself of feelings of attachment and keep your heart open. People open their hearts to advice when it comes from someone who accepts them just as they are. When you are trying to get others to open their hearts to you, you must open your own heart to them.

> "Revealed" means that first a person's eyes are opened, for if his eyes are closed, he will be unable to see anything. His eyes are opened to the fact that all human beings possess the buddha-nature. (*Shinshaku Hokke Sambu-kyo* [New Commentary on the Threefold Lotus Sutra], vol. 8, p. 109)

The founder's trademarks were his open heart and smiling countenance; he was known for these features all over Japan, and everyone he met outside Japan also recognized them.

Someone once described his smile by saying, "He was not exactly smiling because he was happy or enjoying himself—it was a smile that seemed to spring up from deep inside him. The founder's spirit was smiling." I feel that describes it exactly. Whenever memories of the founder well up in my mind, no matter what their context, I am always left with the impression that he was smiling.

> I am often asked why I am able to keep on smiling no matter what happens. There is no particular secret about why I am smiling. My smile is my true reality. The Buddha is a smile. (*Tada Hitasurani* [Only Single-Mindedly], p. 35)

The founder's smiling face was not a mere personal trademark. The founder's warm smile penetrated and opened all hearts. With our hearts thus opened, it is now our turn to open the hearts of those around us and communicate that warmth with our own smiles and words.

It is up to us to make a smiling face the trademark not just of the founder but of all Rissho Kosei-kai members.

What is it that the Buddha is teaching us through the Lotus Sutra? Its point is to "bring liberation to all"; its great declaration is that "all people who hear this sutra will surely be liberated [freed from suffering]." The important thing is to firmly embrace the Buddha's desire for our liberation, which is his compassion. (*San Reizan Meiso* [Meditations from Three Holy Mountains], p. 14)

The founder met everyone without timidity, yet without self-importance. He always opened his own heart, accepted other people, and learned from them.

The true teaching quite naturally flows into any heart as open as the founder's. I hope we can follow in his footsteps and have hearts that are wide open.

# 8  Knowing the Buddha's Compassion
## *The Original Vow of the Buddha*

The Buddha says in the Lotus Sutra, "Ever making this my thought: How can I make living beings / Obtain entry into the unsurpassable Way / And quickly accomplish embodiment as buddhas?" The Buddha makes his appearance in our world to pursue his wish that everyone should enter the Buddha Way and quickly attain the same state of mind as the Buddha enjoys. That is the Buddha's original vow.

—*San Reizan Meiso* (Meditations from Three Holy Mountains)

Founder Nikkyo Niwano said, "The Buddha is always near us; we need only to awaken to this presence, accept his compassion directly with an open mind, and always act in accordance with the Buddha's spirit."

Chapter 2 of the Lotus Sutra, "Skillful Means," tells of how the Buddha made a vow to lead all people into a state of mind without delusion, like his own, and to help us attain a happy mental condition that allows us to lead our entire lives in contentment.

Also, chapter 16 of the Lotus Sutra, "The Eternal Life of the

Tathagata," tells us that the Buddha knows what we have been able to do and what we could not do, what suffering we have faced and how we have tried to overcome it, and that he is always sending us messages in the guise of events perfectly tailored to our circumstances, past and present. It also tells of how he arranges various meetings and encounters that will lead us quickly, easily, and directly to a state of mind like the Buddha's.

> The reason you joined Rissho Kosei-kai was not for the young men's group or men's group activities. What your first wish should be is to fulfill the Buddha's original vow, to attain buddhahood. (Speech at the Great Sacred Hall, Tokyo, November 15, 1985)

In April 1986, a major catastrophe occurred when the Chernobyl nuclear power reactor in Ukraine exploded. Huge amounts of radioactivity were released and spread over a wide area, and high radiation levels were detected in vegetables, water, and mother's milk even in Japan.

The news media reported on this event day after day, filling my mother with apprehension to the point where she asked the founder, "What is to become of us? Will we survive? What shall we do?"

To this the founder promptly replied, "Do not worry. The best thing we can do is to put all of our energy into devoting ourselves to the Buddhist faith. For us, devotion to the Buddha Way is everything."

If we experience any type of major disaster beyond our control, including a nuclear reactor accident, our human-centered vision can see no meaning in it, and we tend to despair.

The founder tells us without hesitation that when we are faced with such a situation, we should not worry but should keep on believing in the Buddha's original vow and focus squarely on that without wavering, and that the most important thing is to go on living. Isn't that the real meaning of truly acceding to the wish of the Eternal Original Buddha?

> The principal and most crucial point of religious training in Buddhism is "crossing a bridge over the river of suffering from birth, old age, sickness, and death." We begin with our birth, our flesh sometimes suffers from illness, we age as the years pass, and we finally die. . . . All things possessing life eventually experience death. We cannot escape this aspect of our own existence, nor is it one for which we can hold others responsible; it is something we must work out for ourselves. The Buddha used the phrase "crossing a bridge over the river of suffering" in the sense of overcoming one's troubles and difficulties. (*Kosei,* April 1966, p. 11)

All people originally have the same spirit as the Buddha, and we are living now for the purpose of expressing it. The Buddha is willing us to express that spirit and give it life; to this end he provides us with encounters and opportunities to do so. Still, we continue to live deluded by superficial elements of good and evil, driven aimlessly by the immediately apparent phenomena of the world. However, the truth is that everything that happens to us is necessary for us in the here and now.

All events must happen just as they do to enable our inherent buddha-nature to shine forth, and all circumstances of our lives are nothing but fortunate karmic conditions conducive to our attainment of buddhahood. All are necessary divine arrangements without which our buddha-nature cannot shine forth. All we need to do is to believe that everything is an expression of the Buddha's compassion.

It is this kind of faith in the Buddha's compassion that allows us to truly accept the promise of the Buddha's original vow.

If we are firmly rooted in such faith, the wall of delusions and defilements that surrounds us will cease to be a barrier even though it remains; it will become permeable, as it were. The buddha-nature that was closed off by that wall will come into direct contact with the compassion of the Eternal Original Buddha and become one with it. In this way, the Buddha's compassion can work to the full within us. (*Shinshaku Hokke Sambu-kyo* [New Commentary on the Threefold Lotus Sutra], vol. 6, p. 100)

## 9 The Necessary Arrangement of All Things
### *Skillful Means*

I think we should not only think of all things that trouble the human heart as skillful means arranged by the Buddha for leading us all to the true Dharma but also awaken to the fact that this proceeds entirely from the Buddha's profound compassion.

—*Kosei,* March 1955

When asked to sum up the teaching of Rissho Kosei-kai as briefly as possible, Nikkyo Niwano, the founder, always promptly answered, "Attain buddhahood."

Once a baby boy was born deaf to a young couple who were members. The mother accepted the situation after receiving confirmation from doctors, thought of her child as a gift from the Buddha, and assumed that her task was simply to raise the boy with love. However, the father wondered why this had to happen to them and how they were to raise the boy, so he took his concern to a leader of his Dharma center.

He was told that his torment about his son could be a penalty for his lack of filial devotion toward his own parents. In fact, he had left his hometown at an early age and caused his parents a lot of worry; perhaps, he thought, he had not been a dutiful son. Now that he was a parent himself, he could finally understand what his own parents must have felt; perhaps the time had come for him to say he was sorry for his behavior. Now there seemed to be a reason he could understand for what had happened. He did not really believe this deep down inside, however, and his heart was still heavy.

> Although there is only one Truth, when it works in and around living people, it takes a variety of forms. An understanding of skillful means allows you to precisely capture these forms. (*Niwano Nikkyo Howa Senshu* [Selected Dharma Talks of Nikkyo Niwano], special volume, p. 133)

The father of the deaf boy finally took his concern to the founder, who told him simply, "You and your wife should raise your son and by doing so become buddhas."

These words from the founder opened his eyes completely. "That is the answer," he thought. "We are living in this world in order to become buddhas. Everything that happens to us in our lives, including having a son born deaf, happens so that we can become buddhas." With this awakening, the father gained a profound understanding of the meaning of his fate.

In the same way that his wife accepted the baby as a gift from the Buddha, he would raise his son with love and attain buddhahood. But the goal of attaining buddhahood must be embraced with a pure heart, he realized. With this awakening, he understood that what his Dharma center leader had said was true after all, and so he thought it would be worthwhile to look back on his own life and atone for his errors.

We cannot learn the Truth without being able to see "skillful means" as temporary phenomena that appear through the interaction of causes and conditions. (*Niwano Nikkyo Howa Senshu* [Selected Dharma Talks of Nikkyo Niwano], special volume, p. 135)

The founder later spoke to the man one more time, saying, "The reasons may still seem obscure to you, but I hope you will raise your son to know true happiness and do so with a completely sincere heart. If you do that, you will eventually understand the real meaning of what has happened to you."

Later, the boy was bullied by other children because of his deafness, and the family faced difficulty in choosing a school and later finding a job for their son, but every time they came up against problems, they remembered what the founder had said and were able to approach their trials as ways and means to facilitate their journey toward buddhahood. Under the guidance of his parents' deep love, the boy never missed a day of school, was able to enter a university, found a job after graduation, and is now working.

With a heart filled with nothing but great mercy and compassion, the Eternal Original Buddha is continually praying that we and all living beings will as soon as possible awaken to the Truth, be enlightened, and attain true peace of mind. (*Niwano Nikkyo Howa Senshu* [Selected Dharma Talks of Nikkyo Niwano], special volume, p. 51)

Perhaps the real reason this couple had a deaf child is that the Buddha arranged this to lead the parents and others who met the boy toward true happiness.

"Skillful means" are all of those chance opportunities that fit the time, place, and individual together so that the person is led toward the Truth. If we assume that all the events of our lives are in fact skillful means, striving to make the best of them is to live in accordance with the wishes of the Buddha and progress on the path toward Truth. When we truly understand the wishes of the Buddha, we become capable of overcoming all the problems that present themselves to us.

> When we worship the gods and the buddhas we recite, "We earnestly ask you to arrange everything for us." By this we are saying, "As you wish, whether it is good or bad," meaning that we pledge to accept whatever arrangements the Buddha makes for us. . . . The time will come when we can realize that everything has been a divine arrangement if we take the long-term view. (*Shabyo Mui* [Transferring the Dharma Water without Losing a Drop], p. 259)

# 10 Liberation through the Truth
*Faith*

The teaching of Buddhism is not some superficial thing that advocates any means available to liberate people from their immediately pressing suffering and trouble. At all events it teaches "liberation based on Truth."

—*Niwano Nikkyo Howa Senshu*
(Selected Dharma Talks of Nikkyo Niwano)

Founder Nikkyo Niwano believed utterly in the Truth as taught in the Lotus Sutra.

Most of us tend to separate our thinking, taking the attitude: "The teachings of the Lotus Sutra are the ideal; real life is another, more difficult matter. The ideal and the real are two different things." We still end up thinking of things in terms of our own personal values or in light of our own experience and thus are unable to see the world of the Lotus Sutra. In fact, we do not really try to see it.

Experience usually teaches us that when we do something good, something good happens to us in return. However, when we do a good deed and our situation improves a bit, we feel glad, but if some intractable problem arises, we become upset. We simply go on telling ourselves and hoping to see it proven that, though we can't be sure, things do seem to be improving. It seems to me we could do a lot better than simply repeat empty reassurances and assume that is what constitutes faith.

The world of the truth of the Lotus Sutra is a world of complete emancipation, the root and the cause.

> The focus of devotion for Rissho Kosei-kai members is the Eternal Buddha Shakyamuni as the embodiment of the eternal life that continues from the past and present and into the future and animates every living being. We ask members to think long and hard about the meaning of this and to sharply focus their faith upon it. (*San Reizan Meiso* [Meditations from Three Holy Mountains], p. 140)

I once knew about a married woman who was constantly running around seeking to help others and whose greatest pleasure lay in leading others to the faith. At that time she had a teenage daughter who had been refusing to go to high school for a few years. She said to herself, "All that I am doing is for my daughter's sake. If I do good for others, everything should turn out all right." So, from early in the morning until late at night, she was always on the go.

When the mother received guidance from her Dharma center leader and determined to try putting it into practice, her daughter would begin going to school again, but after a short while she would stop. This was repeated over and over.

Because the mother was busily performing good deeds, she took it for granted that the source of her problem lay elsewhere and sometimes placed the blame on her husband. No matter how hard she tried, her daughter simply would not be cured of her habit of staying home from school. She even started to have harsh feelings toward the girl.

> The safest and most secure state is when we are being protected by the gods and the buddhas. What do we have to do so that the gods and the buddhas will protect us? All we need to do is maintain ourselves in a state of mind in which we can receive the protection of the gods and the buddhas. (*Niwano Nikkyo Howa Senshu* [Selected Dharma Talks of Nikkyo Niwano], vol. 4, p. 133)

One day, the Dharma center minister addressed the troubled housewife:

"What do you like to do best?" he asked her.

"Dissemination activity!" she replied.

"Well, then, what do you dislike most?"

"Housework. I don't do very much housework."

Hearing this, the minister said, "So, you are basically doing what you like. Like mother, like daughter."

Her daughter was not going to school just because she didn't want to, while she herself was performing bodhisattva practice for the benefit of others—did that mean they were alike?

When she went home that night, she spoke to her daughter and asked her, "What grade would you give me as a mother?" The daughter immediately replied, "I would give you a zero." Naturally, the mother lost heart but resolved to do better and get better marks from her daughter. She began devoting more time and attention to the girl, coming home earlier and giving more attention to the housework she disliked. Day by day, her daughter started giving her better marks—five points, twenty points, forty points.

One day the woman sat down and asked her daughter, "What about yourself? What grade do you give yourself?" The daughter replied, "I get the same as you. When you get zero, I get zero. When you get twenty points, I get twenty points." The mother suddenly realized that her "good-for-nothing" daughter actually possessed the same acute sensitivity as her minister, whom she admired greatly and who had said "like mother, like daughter." "This girl is really something," she thought to herself. It was the first time she had truly thought anything like this about her daughter, and indeed she felt that she had come into contact with the girl's buddha-nature.

From that moment onward, wherever she was, her daughter was never far from her caring thoughts. Because until then she had been a distant mother and had never really had such thoughts before, she was also happy to discover that she had such warm feelings inside and felt her own buddha-nature budding into bloom.

> When faith enables a direct connection with the Eternal Original Buddha, only then will it begin to take shape as true liberation. (*Niwano Nikkyo Howa Senshu* [Selected Dharma Talks of Nikkyo Niwano], vol. 3, p. 124)

Around this time, a cousin came to visit and said to the daughter, "If you want to go to college, you first have to graduate from high school."

At that time, the girl did not seem to react particularly to this information, but the following day she suddenly started attending classes. She never missed another day at school.

What brought about this turn of events? The Eternal Original Buddha wants us to discover the buddha-nature in others and in ourselves; this is what is expected of us in this life and is what allows us to "graduate." Whatever happens after that is up to the Buddha.

> When we have faith, we can resonate directly with the Buddha's heart. If we sincerely believe in the compassion of the Eternal Original Buddha, its power immediately begins working within us. This is the action of resonance, and it is the shortest path to buddhahood. (*Shinshaku Hokke Sambukyo* [New Commentary on the Threefold Lotus Sutra], vol. 6, p. 99)

> Once we realize that the Buddha's legacy (his teaching) is ours for the asking and are willing to receive it, any one of us can swiftly attain enlightenment. (*Shinshaku Hokke Sambukyo* [New Commentary on the Threefold Lotus Sutra], vol. 6, p. 88)

There is a limit to what humans can do. It is close to impossible for us by ourselves to solve every problem or to compel people to change who do not want to change. The best we can do is create good encounters and have a positive effect.

When we become able to see the buddha-nature in others, our immediate problems begin to unfold themselves and tend toward a solution. When this happens, we no longer need to try to reform others or solve problems, because we now see everything as opportunities for our inner light to shine forth.

The difficulties we face also arise from the Buddha's compassion, because they lead us to seek a deeper understanding of the Dharma, thus guiding us to a truly tranquil state of mind.

Because all of our encounters can enable us to learn more of the working of the Buddha, when we can discern the Buddha in our problems and in other people, we can begin to think of the Buddha as acting in our behalf. If we live in consonance with the Truth, the teaching of the Buddha will bring us good results in the form of liberation. That is the world of Truth taught by the Lotus Sutra, which can liberate us completely, down to our roots. That is the essence of true faith.

> What exactly is liberation, anyway? I believe that it boils down to what gives each person true peace of mind and the will to live with hope. Thus, naturally, the form it takes and the manner in which it is achieved depend on the individual and the situation, and thus both are infinitely variable. (*Kosei,* March 1976, p. 11)

Life is difficult at certain times for everyone. There can be no such thing as a completely carefree life. Achieving the attainment of liberation is not going to make your life suddenly carefree, starting tomorrow. That is because it is inevitably necessary for us to experience our suffering in our present time and place. "Liberation" can result from the trouble and suffering we are now going through.

> The important thing is to have faith no matter what. Believe in the Buddha, believe in his teaching, and believe in yourself as someone who consistently desires the happiness of others. (*Yakushin* [Progress], October 1981, p. 14)

The founder has said, "Buddhism is not about the Buddha liberating us; it teaches us to free ourselves through our own deeds." But that does not mean we can figure out how to do this in our own way and achieve it by ourselves.

We may speak of liberating ourselves through our own actions, but this only happens when our spirits resonate with the wishes of the Buddha. When we enter the Buddhist path desiring to take even a baby step closer to the Buddha, that is when the world of liberation and being freed opens up to us.

When you try to do it yourself, somehow you come up against obstacles and experience difficulties, but when you sincerely contemplate the protection of the gods and the buddhas, and that divine protection comes to you, everything works out in ways that can seem positively miraculous. As you gain more and more experience in how wonderfully well things can work out when you come under the protection of the gods and the buddhas, your ego-based self will gradually subside. (*Hosshin* [Raising Aspirations], April 1986, p. 17)

## 11 Born with a Wish
### *Birth by Aspiration*

To receive guidance is not as easy as it seems, and such an encounter with the Buddha does not happen in just a day or two. It occurs as a result of the profound course of our karmic affiliation with the Buddha from previous existences. It is true that since we aspired to the knowledge and insight of the Tathagata [Buddha] and accepted our own inclination to follow up with wholehearted devotion, we joined Rissho Kosei-kai as a result.

*—Niwano Nikkyo Howa Senshu*
(Selected Dharma Talks of Nikkyo Niwano)

One time when Founder Nikkyo Niwano was visiting America, he dropped in at a local Dharma center of Rissho Kosei-kai and had the opportunity to meet with some of the members.

Among the members in the United States at that time were a large number of Japanese women who had married American servicemen in the years immediately following World War II and had moved to the home country of their husbands. Many of them made the trip to America with high hopes, but after their arrival problems developed from the differences in language and culture, and some of the women became estranged from their husbands and eventually resorted to divorce. They also had difficulties raising their children under such circumstances, and many found problems in their lives coming one after another.

Having joined Rissho Kosei-kai and carried out their training, they nevertheless felt distressed every day, fearing that the reason they were now leading such lonely lives far away from Japan was because of some failing in themselves. "What did we do wrong? Was it a failure of filial devotion to our parents?" was a common concern.

To those members who confided their feelings, the founder had the following to say: "I think of all of you as bodhisattvas. To be trying to spread the word of the Lotus Sutra in America while bearing such heavy burdens of personal troubles, you must be great bodhisattvas who were born aspiring to convey the teachings."

These words from the founder caused many of these members in the United States to break into tears. Feeling rewarded for their difficult lives, they warmly wept tears of relief. When they awakened to the state of mind that recognized they must have aspired to be born into this world, their trials, sorrows, and pressing difficulties were all transformed into guidance arising from the Buddha's compassion.

The merit from having paid homage to a trillion buddhas allows us to be born as human beings. Whether or not we can achieve true liberation depends on our realization of how precious such human life is and our awakening to our destiny and mission. (*Gudo* [Search for the Way], December 1971, p. 368)

In chapter 10 of the Lotus Sutra, "A Teacher of the Dharma," it is written, "These people have already paid homage to ten myriad *kotis*\* of buddhas and under the buddhas performed their great vows; therefore, out of compassion for all living beings, they are born here among men."

When we look at human beings with the eyes of the founder, who deeply believed without any doubts in the truth of the Lotus Sutra, we can see all people as children of the Buddha and as having been born with the aspiration to bring others to liberation.

This does not mean: "You aspired to be born, so you simply have to bear whatever suffering comes your way." When you stop searching for causes as the reason that you have to deal with difficulties and suffering and instead look toward your aspiration as the reason, you can then regard even the troubles you encounter as perhaps even clearer evidence that you were born because you have that aspiration. This way of thinking may be the path to achieving your own liberation.

> We can say that whether one has been born into this world as a result of karma or as a result of aspiration is determined by one's degree of self-realization. (*Shinshaku Hokke Sambukyo* [New Commentary on the Threefold Lotus Sutra], vol. 2, p. 336)

If we want to have a more realistic view of the concept of having "paid homage to ten myriad *kotis* of buddhas" in our past lives, we should think of this as referring not only to past lives but also to being able to see every person we have met along the way during our present lives as in reality being a buddha.

---

\* A *koti* is an astronomical number variously interpreted as ten million, one hundred million, and so on.

To have paid homage to a trillion buddhas means to have made the most of ourselves in our encounters with others. It means that everything we have done to survive in life is connected to the path that leads to attaining buddhahood.

## 12  Living as the Buddha Would Wish
### *Training*

The important thing is to realize at all times that we are "being sustained by the Buddha" and to always be prepared to "live in a way that embodies full recognition of the circumstance of being sustained."

—*Niwano Nikkyo Howa Senshu*
(Selected Dharma Talks of Nikkyo Niwano)

Founder Nikkyo Niwano said, "A person cannot be too happy. When you are happy, you should share the merit with others because that multiplies the happiness."

The first step is to communicate to others the joy you feel in your heart when you encounter those small delights and happy moments of everyday life. No matter how minor the occasion for doing this, expressing your joy to others in words can have an astonishing influence upon warming the social atmosphere and encourage happiness. In doing this, you can also develop a deeper feeling for the Dharma taught to us by the Buddha.

The human spirit naturally yearns to advance to the point of attaining buddhahood. We live in this world for the purpose of training our spirits toward that end. (*Niwano Nikkyo Howa Senshu* [Selected Dharma Talks of Nikkyo Niwano], special volume, p. 225)

The purpose of training and discipline is to be happy, to be able to truly feel happiness. We train ourselves not because we have to as members of Rissho Kosei-kai but because such discipline always helps us and sustains us in leading a happy life.

True faith will never arise when there is no questioning of why we are being sustained as we are by something immense. (*Niwano Nikkyo Howa Senshu* [Selected Dharma Talks of Nikkyo Niwano], special volume, p. 62)

We can continue to live even though we may be suffering and confused, all the while giving voice to our complaints and resenting other people. But such a life will be a hard one, without joy. That is why the founder taught us how we can speedily, and without distracting detours, enter the path toward attaining buddhahood and becoming truly happy.

"Try putting yourself second and serve others. Try appreciating your parents. Try finding time in your busy day to recite the sutra. When these things start to come naturally to you, you can live with peace of mind, and your life will be one containing many joys."

This is the good medicine the founder prescribed for us.

Action, however, is in all instances a method for communicating the spirit. The outcome of the exercise actually depends totally on the spirit.

The greatest purpose of the teaching of a manifest-body buddha is to help living beings realize the true way of looking at things, to open their eyes to the Truth. This is the very foundation of liberation. (*Shinshaku Hokke Sambu-kyo* [New Commentary on the Threefold Lotus Sutra], vol. 4, p. 241)

What the founder showed us through his life was how the "training" of the Lotus Sutra enables us to discover our own buddha-nature and the buddha-nature of others. Training is like a ticket that can convey all of us together to our destination with the speed of light. This ticket that the founder gave us is like a transfer allowing us to change from a train or bus to a vehicle traveling at fantastic speed.

The training of the Lotus Sutra can appear simply idealistic from the perspective of worldly common sense, but when we believe in its efficacy and let ourselves flow with the current leading toward the single point that is the wish of the Buddha—manifestation of our buddha-nature—beyond a doubt the outcome will be something we could not previously imagine.

The three basic religious practices—sutra recitation; participating in dissemination, guidance, and *hoza* sessions; and study and practice of the Dharma—train us to live in accordance with the wishes of the Eternal Original Buddha, that is, to discover our buddha-nature through such actions.

You are sadly mistaken if you think you can obtain some merit when you have burned so many sticks of incense and sat down one morning to diligently read the Lotus Sutra for a few hours. What counts is careful examination of the meaning of its content and applying what you have digested in your own life. (*Niwano Nikkyo Howa Senshu* [Selected Dharma Talks of Nikkyo Niwano], special volume, p. 148)

There is the case of a married couple who, soon after the wife was diagnosed as having leukemia, learned that she was pregnant. The fact of her pregnancy brought joy to the couple, but now they were uncertain whether they would be able to raise a child under the circumstances and, indeed, were afraid that the wife might endanger her own life in giving birth. Together they asked the founder for his advice.

"The first thing to do is to pray for others' happiness. In other words, as a couple you should bring the teaching of the Buddha to others who are in a situation similar to yours."

To live for the happiness of others while you are still suffering and confused is something that might be hard to conceive for many people.

However, in this way the founder taught the couple how to discover the happiness that cannot be taken away and to live fulfilling lives.

The pair accepted the founder's words and determined to convert their difficulty into the treasure of their lives and made their reason for living the work of bringing the teaching to others in their own situation.

All people repeatedly taste both joy and sorrow in their lives. When we are faced with difficulties, we hastily embrace training practices simply to relieve our anxiety and suffering, repeating this cycle until our lives have ended.

Really liberating people means helping them to awaken to the true way to live.

Praying to the gods and the buddhas to ask them to intercede and change something is usually not real prayer. Praying to live in accordance with the wishes of the gods and the buddhas is what is important. (*Tada Hitasurani* [Only Single-Mindedly], p. 32)

Living in accordance with the Buddha's wishes means that we need only think of any suffering and difficulty as necessary effort and compassionate practice. When even one person thinks so, that in itself becomes the foundation on which happiness can grow. In the midst of life's sorrows and joys, people come into contact with others and begin to support each other through interaction. Through such encounters and contacts with others, we can train ourselves in compassionate practice so as to attain happiness.

Sharing our precious merit with others brings out the best in us. Living itself becomes training, and I think we can call this liberation.

Training is no more, and no less, than the effort you put into developing the strength of spirit that keeps you from being discouraged no matter what sorrows or ill fortune befall you and allows you to correctly overcome whatever problems you may encounter. (*Niwano Nikkyo Howa Senshu* [Selected Dharma Talks of Nikkyo Niwano], special volume, p. 144)

## 13 Revealing Buddha-Nature in Everyone
### *Bodhisattva Practice*

The bodhisattva practice originates with revering others, that is, with our recognizing the buddha-nature of all people. If we try to [liberate] others without recognizing their buddha-nature, we only perform empty and formal deeds. True [liberation] lies in our disclosing of and respect for the buddha-nature innate in others.

*—Buddhism for Today*

Founder Nikkyo Niwano taught us that bodhisattva practice begins with the desire to bring all people to the awareness that they are sustained by the Buddha and are children of the Buddha.

A bodhisattva is a messenger from the Buddha. As a child of the Buddha and a messenger from the Buddha, a bodhisattva venerates all people in the same way as the Buddha, sees their buddha-nature, and discovers the Buddha within each person. This is the bodhisattva way of life. Thus, true bodhisattva practice functions as a condition that causes the flower of buddha-nature to bloom. It awakens in others a wish to adopt for themselves the same way of life.

All of us are walking along the Buddha's path. We are living in place of the Buddha. We are the Buddha's hands and feet. (*Niwano Nikkyo Howa Senshu* [Selected Dharma Talks of Nikkyo Niwano], special volume, p. 152)

A person who is clearly aware that life's purpose is reaching the goal of "attaining buddhahood" and whose spirit is in complete accord with this awareness is a bodhisattva. Concrete actions that manifest this awareness in the course of everyday life constitute bodhisattva practice.

People who recognize not only all the troubles that everyone experiences as bodhisattva practice but also the true nature deep within themselves as the brilliantly shining buddha-nature are bodhisattvas.

The most important thing for such bodhisattvas is the spirit of loving and benefiting others, and the practical action that springs from that spirit. This action is called "donation." (*Shinshaku Hokke Sambu-kyo* [New Commentary on the Threefold Lotus Sutra], vol. 8, p. 26)

A mother in Japan had a grown son who chose to stay indoors at home and who had not gone outside for several years. Friends and neighbors knew of the situation and hoped that this long-suffering mother would one day find happiness. They tried everything they could think of to somehow encourage her son to go out and find work.

Let's try to look at this situation from what the founder called the bodhisattva viewpoint. Although the situation involved her own son, this mother truly loved the young man and experienced many difficulties because of him. His existence to that point was entirely thanks to his mother's efforts. From this point of view, she

*The author visiting a local Rissho Kosei-kai Dharma center for a meeting with its leaders in January 2008. The large panel behind her is a portrait of Rev. Nikkyo Niwano.*

*The author writing an essay for a Rissho Kosei-kai periodical in her office at the organization's headquarters in Tokyo in February 2008.*

*The author leads members in reciting the Lotus Sutra on New Year's Day 2010 in the Great Sacred Hall at the headquarters of Rissho Kosei-kai in Tokyo.*

*The opening session of the Sixth World Assembly of the World Conference on Religion and Peace (now called the World Conference of Religions for Peace) was held in the Vatican's Synod Hall on November 3, 1994. Rev. Nikkyo Niwano, seated to the left of Pope John Paul II, delivered the opening address.*

*The author at age three visiting the office of Founder Niwano in the Great Sacred Hall on April 5, 1971. The founder is helping his little granddaughter drink Japanese tea.*

*The author in Mindanao, Philippines, where she helped distribute "dream bags" containing toys and school supplies to local children. The Dream Bag Project is held annually by Rissho Kosei-kai, in which cloth bags that are handmade and filled with gifts by members are sent to children in countries suffering from armed conflicts.*

*The author accompanying children and their mothers in a fund-raising drive for UNICEF during Rissho Kosei-kai's annual Youth Day on May 17, 2009.*

was a bodhisattva, and the troubles she went through can be called bodhisattva practice.

> The true value of our existence as children of the Buddha comes forth when compassion is awakened in our hearts and is realized in compassionate acts. (*Niwano Nikkyo Howa Senshu* [Selected Dharma Talks of Nikkyo Niwano], special volume, p. 60)

When the mother's friends and neighbors stopped saying, "What you should do is . . ." or "Here is my suggestion," and started to simply treat her with warmth and respect, all the emotional pain she had felt until then seemed to fade away. With this, her son's state of mind underwent an unexpected change, and of his own accord he went out to look for a job.

The important thing is to faithfully put into actual practice in our own lives and relationships the content of the lesson the founder taught us.

> A bodhisattva is one who has a great will to [liberate] others, and he can certainly [liberate] all living beings suffering from illusion and suffering on specific occasions. Fundamental [liberation], however, is not brought about except by our realization of the existence of the Buddha. (*Buddhism for Today,* p. 378)

The founder taught us about bodhisattva practice by telling us to put others first.

Although we are all, in fact, bodhisattvas on the path toward becoming buddhas, we simply fail to notice this. This is why the founder urged us to start by undertaking bodhisattva practice, telling us, "If you want to be happy, put others first." In this way he made us aware of the bodhisattva spirit that has always resided in us, helping us to awaken it.

Undertaking bodhisattva practice helps us come closer to the bodhisattva spirit.

Once when the founder was visiting a certain Rissho Kosei-kai Dharma center, he met a young man who had just assumed his duties as leader of the Dharma center's young men's group.

The man asked the founder, "I have just become leader of the young men's group—what is the best way for me to fulfill my responsibilities?"

The founder folded his arms across his chest and answered in a strong voice, "Here's what you should do. See to it that someone else becomes even more fascinated by the Lotus Sutra than you are."

After that, the young man fulfilled his duties by keeping his focus constantly on how to communicate the wonder of the Lotus Sutra to others, while carefully studying it himself. He is now the minister of a Dharma center, and in his many encounters with others he uses the words of the founder as the compass for his faith.

> How does a bodhisattva manifest his [liberation] to living beings? This is, of course, a [liberation] revealed by him to [liberate] them from their illusions and suffering on specific occasions. A much more important working of his [liberation], however, is to transmit the Buddha's teachings as his messenger and to provide us with a good example of religious life. (*Buddhism for Today,* p. 378)

One time when the founder was traveling overseas, the father of his male secretary passed away. The secretary's colleagues in Tokyo were going to contact him to tell him to come home, but his mother said, "My son's coming home will not bring his father back. Please let him carry on with the important work he is doing." And so he did not learn of his father's death until he returned to Japan.

Immediately after they returned, the founder visited the secretary's home. Bowing low to the astonished mother, he said, "I regret that your son could not be with you when his father passed away. I am really very sorry."

Hearing of this, the secretary commented, "Without even resting after traveling abroad on the vital task of pursuing world peace, he visited my family home. The sincerity and good faith he showed by this, as he does in all things, is what makes me love and respect him as a father and teacher. It is what enables me to follow him, come what may."

The way the founder put others first, acting with deep sincerity to the point of forgetting about himself, was what led those around him to aspire to enlightenment.

In order to make the world brighter and more peaceful, one has to awaken to the fact that the realization of the buddha-nature within oneself and others is the true starting point and the most basic path. (*Shinshaku Hokke Sambu-kyo* [New Commentary on the Threefold Lotus Sutra], vol. 8, p. 49)

## 14  Casting Light
### *Putting One's Hands Together*

Shakyamuni said very clearly that all living things are endowed with buddha-nature. When we thoroughly grasp this in a tangible way, we will, like the Bodhisattva Never Despise described in chapter 20 of the Lotus Sutra, become unable to refrain from venerating every person we meet and will feel reverence for the person from the heart.

—*Hosshin* (Raising Aspirations), March 1992

While on a pilgrimage to the Enjitsuji temple on Mount Hakii in Yamanashi Prefecture, Founder Nikkyo Niwano visited a nearby Rissho Kosei-kai Dharma center. A meeting was organized for members to receive guidance from the founder, and at the meeting a young woman who was in charge of the activities of high school students of the center raised her hand.

"While I was helping out at the Dharma center, I accidentally injured my little finger. Please tell me in what spirit I should accept this happening to me." In response, the founder broke into a sunny smile and said, "If you are so advanced in your devotions while still so young, by the time you reach my age you'll be a buddha!"

The young woman tried to change herself through recognizing the reason why she had injured her finger. What the founder was communicating here, however, was the great value of a pure heart that seeks to gaze into one's inner spirit through the medium of even such minor things.

The founder's words no doubt helped the young woman touch her buddha-nature. She later noted, "Since that time there have been occasions when I have felt close to being defeated by adversity, but then I remember the founder's smile and words and continue my religious practice."

> The reason we place our hands together in a prayerful attitude when we exchange ordinary greetings such as "Good morning" or expressions of gratitude such as "Thanks for your trouble" is to more perfectly refine and bring out the buddha-nature that each of us has inside. (*Niwano Nikkyo Howa Senshu* [Selected Dharma Talks of Nikkyo Niwano], vol. 3, p. 211)

The founder always put his hands together when greeting every person he met, including all of his family members, even us grandchildren. When he was near us, we always found that our happiest feelings would well up inside us and we would become hopeful and eager to please others. It was not so much that the founder did not blame us if we did something wrong, or that he forgave us, but that he was always able to find within us and bring out the Buddha spirit that we ourselves could not see and cast light upon it.

One day when our family was holding sutra recitation service, the founder was officiating, and I thought that the pace at which he was reading was too slow and that I would not be able to leave the house when I was supposed to, and though I realized it was unkind, I tried to hasten the pace of the recitation. Naturally my voice grew louder.

When the greatly speeded-up service ended, the founder's entire face beamed in a big smile as he looked behind him, and he said, "Well, today's service was certainly vigorous—now, that was great sutra recitation!" And though I felt embarrassed and regretful for not following the founder's pace, his words made me glad. This was not because I had not been cautioned about not following his pace. It was because, like a magician, the founder had suddenly pulled out and showed me the buddha-nature within me of which I myself had not been aware.

No matter with whom you are dealing, if you truly want to guide someone to the Dharma, you must embrace a feeling of respect for that person. When you greet all of those you meet with your hands placed together, this shows that you trust them and believe in their buddha-nature and the spirit of the Buddha that resides in their true self, thus you are showing your deepest reverence for their character. As seen with particular clarity in the way the Lotus Sutra describes how the Bodhisattva Never Despise revered all people he met, the act of greeting every single person with your hands placed together serves as a means and opportunity for awakening the aspiration to supreme enlightenment in that person. (*Hosshin* [Raising Aspirations], June 1986, p. 16)

When we grandchildren rang the bell or beat the Buddhist wooden block during sutra recitation, the founder would always be pleased and tell us, "Great sound! You did that well." At mealtimes he would praise the preparation of the food, saying, "Meals at our house are the best in the world!" He always communicated a great warmth that arose from his way of seeing only the best in people, seeing only their Buddhist heart. Thus, when the founder was present, we never worried about anything and always felt secure. A sudden feeling of warmth would arise in us whenever we thought about how we would always like to be someone who could please the founder.

> The Buddha appeared in the world to help all people attain buddhahood, and our faith in Buddhism occurs so that we can accept the wish of the Buddha without cynicism and contribute to each and every person's growth toward becoming a buddha. This is why we wonder how we can achieve the same state of mind as the Buddha and seek to know what to do in order to attain buddhahood. (*San Reizan Meiso* [Meditations from Three Holy Mountains], p. 16)

## 15 A Tiny Window Letting in a Beam of Light
### *Revere the Buddha-Nature of Others*

To discover and respect others' buddha-nature is indeed the primary object of the bodhisattva practice, and living Buddhism consists of this.

—*Buddhism for Today*

Founder Nikkyo Niwano has taught us that "to revere buddha-nature is to believe that all people have buddha-nature and to see things in such a way as to discover, in our contact with others, a warm exchange of our mutual buddha-natures."

To revere buddha-nature is to revere others as they are, to respect them. It is to believe from the heart that "the person standing in front of us is someone who enables us to grow spiritually and do our bodhisattva practice"; by putting the palms of our hands together in reverence, we allow the light of the Buddha to shine on the contact and allow others as well as ourselves to become aware of buddha-nature.

The words of one who respects the other are warm words. That warmth imparts hope, joy, and peace of mind to others, creating assurance in the mind.

> It is this: "Revering the buddha-nature of people is the foundation of Buddhist practice and should be given precedence over all else." (*Shinshaku Hokke Sambu-kyo* [New Commentary on the Threefold Lotus Sutra], vol. 8, p. 36)

Once when the founder was on a trip, after he had returned to his lodgings when his business for the day was finished, his secretary thought that the founder must be very tired, and he summoned a shiatsu massage therapist.

The founder had to take a phone call just as the masseur arrived. He insisted that his secretary get a massage first, telling him, "You must be tired, too."

As the massage began, the secretary thought, "Oh, no!" because the masseur was unskilled. He felt that the masseur should not be paid, but it was too late to cancel the massage, and soon it was the founder's turn. As he watched with apologetic concern, however, the situation changed.

When the masseur started working on the area of the founder's lower back, the founder encouraged and praised him, saying, "Just a little bit lower. Yes, that's the spot! A little more pressure now! Good, that's working! You are very good!" In response to the founder's praise, the masseur put his heart and soul into the massage.

> One only has to revere other human beings. One only has to revere buddha-nature. (*Niwano Nikkyo Howa Senshu* [Selected Dharma Talks of Nikkyo Niwano], special volume, p. 58)

The shiatsu session took twice the usual time, and at the end the masseur said, bowing, "I am just a trainee and not yet fully qualified. You have taught me a lot today, and I have learned a great deal. Thank you very much." He did not ask to be paid. But the founder joyfully gave him more than might have been expected, saying, "On the contrary, I received a very good massage from you today."

The secretary was thus once again strongly reminded of the great heart of the founder, who could bring out the best in anyone he met at any time by showing reverence for the person.

> If we boil down the philosophical principles of the teachings of the Buddha to their absolute essence, what is left? We are left with the truth that "all living beings are endowed with buddha-nature." How can anyone and everyone easily act upon this truth in their daily lives? By fixing their eyes upon the buddha-nature within themselves and looking reverently upon the buddha-nature within others. (*Shinshaku Hokke Sambu-kyo* [New Commentary on the Threefold Lotus Sutra], vol. 8, p. 12)

We all share lives of the same basic nature and are children of the Buddha. Our abilities and personalities may have various superficial differences, but we are all equal in being the Buddha's children and sustained in life, while all possessing buddha-nature. It was the founder's wish that we be able to overcome our superficial differences and recognize the buddha-nature in a person, to see that tiny window letting in a beam of light.

To show reverence for the buddha-nature in others, we should become people who can focus our attention on their kindness, the mind of the Buddha that they have within themselves. It can be troublesome to meet people who do not behave as we would like, people who do not listen to what they are being told, and people who in general are difficult to get along with. But taking the necessary trouble helps us to understand ourselves and to grow.

> We try to find the tiny window in others' minds; we respect it as far as possible; and by doing so, we make others become aware of it themselves. A person who realizes the existence of the tiny window in his own mind will open it wider for himself because he desires to let more light enter the depths of his mind. This is the meaning of disclosing and respecting others' buddha-nature and at the same time discovering one's own buddha-nature. (*Buddhism for Today*, p. 311)

If we think about the vow of the Eternal Original Buddha, we can agree that the entire world surrounding us is a manifestation of buddha-nature. It is difficult to personally experience from the start, however, that "everything is a manifestation of buddha-nature." That is why we begin by first discovering that "tiny window of light." In reality, we must first detect a gleam before we can realize that it is something ablaze and recognize it as light.

The founder has said, "We encounter the Buddha every day. The Buddha, as buddha-nature, is in everyone, and so buddha-nature is in us. When we encounter another person, buddha-nature to buddha-nature, we will see that person as the Buddha, no matter what sort of individual he or she is, and we will be able to look upon the person with reverence." If someone meets another person with palms placed together in reverence and thinks, "The Buddha is making use of this person" and "This person is enabling me to show my buddha-nature clearly," it will be like the simple praying of the Bodhisattva Never Despise. But how did the founder act on this and put it into practice?

During a meeting held in advance of the Sixth World

Assembly of the World Conference of Religions for Peace in 1994, an unpleasant argument broke out over a mistake in the reference materials. The air in the conference room was filled with tension. The founder raised his hand and said the following:

"I want to thank you for your spirited discussion of these valuable materials. The fact is, my eyesight is not very good anymore, so I can't properly read them. My hearing is also not very good, to the point that I haven't been able to completely follow your arguments. But if there is anything I can do for you, don't hesitate to ask."

The founder did not rebuke the group for the fact that the meeting had become disorderly, nor did he place the blame on anyone. He bowed deeply, showing reverence for all in the meeting room, and the atmosphere changed completely. Constructive discussions soon followed.

> The Buddha says with conviction and at length that if we show reverence for the buddha-nature in each other and strive to walk the path of the bodhisattva, the entire world will be filled with the light of the newly discovered and polished buddha-nature. (*Kosei,* July 1966, p. 15)

As is stated in chapter 20 of the Lotus Sutra, "The Bodhisattva Never Despise," "And age by age meeting buddhas / They will speedily accomplish the Buddha Way," we will experience happiness and become buddhas by recognizing the Buddha in everyone we meet each day.

If all people are the Buddha's children, then those I meet are all buddhas. When the mind thinks that way, with respect, it is on the path to buddhahood, the Buddha Way. When one person respects another, that will lead to caring words and compassionate behavior.

If we put this the other way around, we can say that if a person is speaking with caring words and acting compassionately, that person is showing reverence for the buddha-nature in others. The reverential acts of the Bodhisattva Never Despise are the acts through which oneself and another can both attain buddhahood.

Creating many bodhisattvas, which is in accord with the Buddha's original vow, is the true mission of Rissho Kosei-kai. (*Niwano Nikkyo Howa Senshu* [Selected Dharma Talks of Nikkyo Niwano], vol. 2, p. 153)

## 16 The Peacemakers
### *Cooperation among Religions*

We can sum up the meaning of the peace movement among people of faith as being for the purpose of "becoming a buddha." This means that each individual engages in training to attain buddhahood and calls out to many others to attain buddhahood themselves. If we forget this basic, underlying purpose, no amount of campaigning will bring true peace to our world.

—*Yakushin* (Progress), March 1982

Founder Nikkyo Niwano declared, "I will travel anywhere for the purpose of world peace and interreligious cooperation." These were not idle words: He devoted the latter part of his life to the world peace movement. In 1979, during the hostage crisis at the American Embassy in Tehran, Iran, he traveled to the Middle East to offer himself as a substitute hostage. In 1994 he ignored his advanced age of eighty-eight to attend the Sixth World Assembly of the World Conference of Religions for Peace in Riva del Garda, Italy.

What motivated the founder, why did he devote himself

wholeheartedly to the pursuit of world peace? Of course it was in an attempt to end conflicts and bring harmony to the world. However, I believe that the motivation that brought him to risk his life for this cause was the same thing that motivated him always—his determination to fulfill the Buddha's wish at all times and to revere the buddha-nature in all people.

For the founder, who thoroughly and completely practiced reverence for buddha-nature in the manner of the Bodhisattva Never Despise, taking part in world peace and interreligious cooperation movements was exactly the same thing as revering the buddha-nature in a single person standing right next to him. For him, these movements existed in order to bring to perfection reverence for buddha-nature as practiced by the Bodhisattva Never Despise by applying it to all the people of the world.

I think all of us should follow the founder in this by revering the buddha-nature in others, starting with the person right next to us and, with the purpose of revering all people, extending ourselves to take part in the peace movement.

> The gods and the buddhas are not partial; they do not extend their protection only to one person and not to another. They give their protection to everyone, whoever that may be, in the same way. This is the way it should be among people as well; we should share in the spirit of religious cooperation as a way of esteeming others. (*Hosshin* [Raising Aspirations], May 1990, p. 17)

In 1972 the founder was campaigning for support for the Second World Assembly of the World Conference of Religions for Peace and paid a visit to Bishop Hermann Kunst, who was the representative of the Protestant Evangelische Kirche in Deutschland (Evangelical Church in Germany) to the (then) West German government. As soon as the founder met him, Bishop Kunst asked him quite pointedly, "What qualifies you to come here to us on this errand?" The founder replied, "I have no particular qualifications, nor has any person sent me here. It is at the behest of the Eternal Original Buddha that I am attempting to meet with world leaders." And he shot back a question to Bishop Kunst, "Does not the God in your heaven order you to call people to lead the world to peace?" In reply to this question, Bishop Kunst simply thrust out his big hand and grasped the founder's hand tightly. "Now I understand," he said. "Let us have faith in all you say."

The founder's consistent practice was to devote himself to the wish of the Eternal Original Buddha, who gives life to everything in existence, and thus he did not concern himself with the superficial differences among religions, nor did he criticize the religions of others but accepted and admired them. In this way he showed us that all religions have the same root, which is "All arises from the One Dharma."

> When we speak of world peace, we are speaking of liberation down to the very roots, of the complete liberation of every single being on earth. Thus when we speak of world peace, we are speaking of the final conclusion when true liberation will be found. (*Tada Hitasurani* [Only Single-Mindedly], p. 110)

The First Assembly of the Asian Conference of Religions for Peace (ACRP) was held in Singapore in 1976. At that time, the news media carried reports of Vietnamese fleeing their country in small boats, without sufficient food, threatened by storms, lacking permission to land anywhere, adrift on the high seas, and facing death by starvation.

At this point, even the United Nations had not begun acting

to assist these Vietnamese refugees. The officers of the ACRP and Religions for Peace cooperated on a resolution calling on the international community to lend a helping hand to these people. The reality of the situation was far from simple, however.

Many obstacles existed, such as the international legal difficulties of accepting more than five hundred refugees at a time and the complicated political situation in Asian countries then. The greatest problem of all, however, was lack of funds. Meeting upon meeting was held with no satisfactory outcome, so when every means possible seemed to have been exhausted, members of the Japanese Committee of Religions for Peace held an emergency session.

The founder believed that a solution would definitely be found if only everyone would let their hearts follow the dictates of the gods and the buddhas, and he addressed the meeting saying, "I believe the time has come when we as religious practitioners must 'put the Truth into practice.'" Having thus broached the subject, he made his initial appeal for donations. All participants nodded in approval of the appeal of the founder, and in the end the Japanese Committee of Religions for Peace decided to provide half of the funds needed.

> In these times it is not enough just to think of yourself. Every individual must now think of others, think of the whole planet, and act. (*San Reizan Meiso* [Meditations from Three Holy Mountains], p. 147)

This decision resulted in a solution at the ACRP plenary session, and rescue operations were launched immediately. Moreover, the action taken by these religious leaders proved to be a turning point, after which the United Nations began to assist the refugees in earnest.

In his speech at the conclusion of the ACRP assembly, the founder said, "Religion does not exist in doctrine—it exists in sincere action."

I believe that, for the founder, the peace movement was not an ideal or something ideological but was no more nor less than a clear manifestation of buddha-nature in concrete form and a way to revere the buddha-nature in all the people in the world.

> We have the teaching that all things—mountains, rivers, plants, trees, and indeed all things in existence—can attain buddhahood. The Lotus Sutra tells us that we should recognize the value in all things and allow them to exist. This applies not just to other living beings but also to mountains, rivers, plants, trees, and every single thing in existence, as all have buddha-nature and all partake in the same gift of life. The Lotus Sutra teaches us that rather than resorting to confrontation, we should live allowing each person to make the best of his or her own particular qualities. This is the concept that will bring liberation to our present world. The teaching of the Lotus Sutra is something that can transform a world of confrontation and disputes into one of peace based on cooperation and understanding and at the same time lead humanity toward true happiness. (*San Reizan Meiso* [Meditations from Three Holy Mountains], p. 147)

"If there is even one person who is able to pay reverence to others, the Buddha will certainly bring happiness to us." These are the words of the founder, who truly had faith in people and sincerely believed that true human nature is buddha-nature. The goal of "lasting world peace" that the founder hoped for is part of what he meant when he said this.

All of us are human, and we are all the children of the Buddha.

We all have life and are nothing else but living proof of buddha-nature itself. It is when we are faced with difficulties that we discover whether we truly believe in that buddha-nature and whether we can revere others without restraint.

## 17  A Treasure in the Heart
### Revelation of Buddha-Nature

We do not with our own eyes see everyone's buddha-nature. But through the Buddha's teachings, we can become fully aware that all people have buddha-nature.

—*Shinshaku Hokke Sambu-kyo*
(New Commentary on the Threefold Lotus Sutra)

Founder Nikkyo Niwano said, "When you realize that you are a child of the Buddha, this is what we call 'revelation of buddha-nature.'"

We are all walking on the path toward happiness. What is important to attain happiness is to take the initiative and make the effort to discover the Buddha hidden within the painful aspects of present reality. By making the effort to discover the marvelous treasure we have been granted—that is, our buddha-nature—we are able to create for ourselves a calm, happy life that enriches our hearts and minds.

Even though we possess a treasure, if we do not know that we have it, it will be of no more use to us than if we did not have it.

The realization that we have this treasure is our first step to liberation. With this realization, the world we see around us suddenly changes as if by magic. When we awaken to the fact that, like ourselves, every other person also possesses buddha-nature, our attitude toward these persons also inevitably changes.

One morning at our house, our eldest daughter, then in the second grade, was getting ready to go to school. She glanced at her daily school diary and found the pages covered with scribbling. Her little sister had done this the night before. Our eldest daughter takes good care of her things and likes to keep everything neat and clean, so this was quite a blow to her. She looked very disappointed, but as her little sister was only about eighteen months old, she could not find it in her heart to get angry. As she opened her eyes wide and fought back her tears, I said to her, "I'm sorry. I guess she wanted to try doing homework just like you do. I'm sure she didn't mean any harm. Please forgive her." Still, the scribbles were made with a marker pen and could not be erased, so she simply had to go to school with her diary looking like a mess.

However, when she got to school and as usual opened the diary for her teacher to look at, the teacher said, "What is this? Did your little sister do this? Well, it's a good job!"

And on the page full of scribbles she put a big check mark, stamped it with her "Excellent" rubber stamp, and even applied a sticker reserved for the best work by any pupil that day. Our eldest daughter was astounded.

When she came home and told us all about this, her expression was one of real happiness. She tenderly said to her little sister, "The teacher praised you and said you did a good job! I have been wanting to receive this sticker for a long time—it is not given out so easily, you know. This is really something!" With that, she peeled off the sticker and gave it to her sister. From then on, every time her little sister did something similar, she would praise her by saying, "Good job!" In this way, her teacher helped our eldest daughter discover the treasure in her heart.

> If we approach others with this spirit of tolerance, we will naturally begin to want to help extend their potential. This feeling is what we call compassion. (*Shinshaku Hokke Sambukyo* [New Commentary on the Threefold Lotus Sutra], vol. 8, p. 49)

We are alive to accomplish just one thing, which we do through the medium of all the experiences and encounters of our entire life. That one thing is to discover the treasure in our hearts and reveal it. To realize this in the course of life and make our buddha-nature manifest is the one thing the Buddha wishes for us. Whether we succeed or fail in our various endeavors, whether we are happy or sad and suffering, all are important lessons for us in pursuit of that goal.

The founder said, "Our real job is to manifest our buddha-nature; everything else is just a part-time task." Revealing our buddha-nature in all of our encounters every day is all we really need to do.

Most of us tend to judge things superficially—I said this, or somebody said that to me; I did this, or someone did that to me. However, we need to practice how to look not at the surface but at the heart beneath the surface, and then at the treasure within that heart. All people and things function as tests for determining the progress of our state of mind and as assignments for practicing how to perceive the true nature of other people's hearts.

"All people and things exist for the purpose of revealing buddha-nature." If you have complete faith in this one thing, set your sights upon it, see the world and other people in its light, and act accordingly, then you are on the path toward buddhahood. We are, in fact, all walking together on this path.

> It is important to master the ability to achieve a complete change in your immediate situation by virtue of your own state of mind. When you can do this, you can maintain a heartfelt faith in the Buddha no matter what problems arise, because you can approach such problems thinking, "This has happened because the Buddha is watching over me and testing me with his great mercy and compassion to help me show a greater degree of humanity. This is a most welcome situation!" (*Kosei,* February 1994, p. 13)

The founder said, "The Lotus Sutra does not simply point to itself as sacred writing but shows that whatever can teach people the truth is the Lotus Sutra." If this is true, it also means that there are many bodhisattvas carrying out the work of the Buddha in the world even though they have never encountered the Lotus Sutra. By discovering these bodhisattvas and admiring their virtue, we will cause the treasure in our own hearts to shine a bit more brightly.

## 18 All Can Attain Buddhahood
### *The One Buddha-Vehicle*

The One Buddha-Vehicle means that all the teachings are given to lead all sentient beings to buddhahood.

—*Shinshaku Hokke Sambu-kyo*
(New Commentary on the Threefold Lotus Sutra)

Founder Nikkyo Niwano said, "True faith will not arise unless you wonder why you have been given life." So, why have we been given life?

We have been given life in order to attain buddhahood.

People experience not just happiness in life—we invariably experience trouble, sorrow, and bitterness as well. However, such experiences are not necessarily "bad." Everything we experience is what we need to experience in order to attain buddhahood. There is no doubt that we will attain buddhahood; every person is on the path to buddhahood.

One and the same event can be seen either as a plus or as a minus, and the differences in the way we see and think about something are revealed in our personalities and lives.

The founder said, "When you have faith in the gods and the buddhas and feel 'The buddhas are always beside me, and the gods are always protecting me,' then you can be consistently sincere, calm, and composed. This is the most important quality of faith."

We tend to seek the commonsense forms of happiness and become wrapped up in securing them, suffering pain and confusion in our efforts to solve our problems. But within such suffering, can we discover joy and gratitude in our hearts? This marks an important crossroads on the path to happiness.

To develop the ability to discover the virtue and blessings in any sort of situation, and thus to cultivate the Buddha's wisdom, is the greatest reason we are being given life, and religious training constitutes the practice of focusing our attention on this truth. All change starts when you can achieve such a change of heart and align your spirit in this direction. The result is the ability to live peacefully even through a lifetime filled with great sorrow and suffering.

There are no such situations as "This person can attain buddhahood, but that person cannot" or "You can never be liberated through this or that religious practice." If, by realizing this, you can obtain the eyes to see, you will see that every person is on the way to buddhahood and that every person is a would-be buddha. This is the meaning of the phrase "Not one fails to attain buddhahood" in chapter 2 of the Lotus Sutra, "Skillful Means."

Those who have faith in the Eternal Original Buddha and try to put Buddhist teaching into practice can discern the form of the Eternal Original Buddha and hear the sound of his preaching in everything they see, hear, and experience. (*Honzonkan no Kakuritsu no Tameni* [For Confirming Our View of the Focus of Devotion], p. 68)

One day, at the start of a leadership meeting of Dharma center ministers, one of the ministers immediately raised his hand high and asked the founder's opinion about his problem with a lack of members volunteering for night duty. The founder gave him a warm smile and answered as follows:

"You have a lot of courage to be the first to ask a question in front of everyone about a problem most centers would not like to admit they have. With so much enthusiasm, you will no doubt work things out. I am sure you will receive the Buddha's blessing."

The minister was asking the founder what he should do to encourage more people to sign up for night duty. However, the founder answered not by giving direct advice but by praising his enthusiastic spirit, telling him things would work out all right. Hearing this, the minister realized that although he had been telling others that "all can attain buddhahood," his own spirit had not yet settled into alignment with that thought.

> *Shravakas,* disciples who hear and follow the Buddha's teaching, and *pratyekabuddhas,* those engaged in religious training without a teacher, can become bodhisattvas the moment they aspire resolutely to practice the bodhisattva way of liberating sentient beings. Fundamentally, they have the same human nature as bodhisattvas. (*Shinshaku Hokke Sambu-kyo* [New Commentary on the Threefold Lotus Sutra], vol. 2, p. 276)

Rather than look at the true aspect of reality, we tend to make instant judgments, thinking "This is, or is not, how things should be." We do this when we view daily events as negative phenomena. If, as the founder always did, we learn to discern the greatest possible joy in each present moment, it is possible that we can transform the everyday world into the world of the Buddha just by a single word. It is our own way of looking at things that unnecessarily makes the change difficult to happen.

When problems do occur to us, it is in a sense wasteful to solve them right away. The Buddha's purpose with respect to problem solving does not concern whether we can solve our problems but involves how we approach those problems and how our spirits rise to the occasion.

> Animals, plants, mountains, rivers, and all things existing in nature share equally in the great life of the universe and are manifestations of the Eternal Original Buddha; we arise also from the same life root. This is the essence of the lessons of the Lotus Sutra. (*Niwano Nikkyo Howa Senshu* [Selected Dharma Talks of Nikkyo Niwano], special volume, p. 64)

## 19 Connected to the Buddha's Wishes
### *Great Peace of Mind*

If our mind is awakened to its original, true nature (buddha-nature), the world in which all human beings, all other living things, and all matter exist in great harmony (the Land of Tranquil Light) appears.

—*Shinshaku Hokke Sambu-kyo*
(New Commentary on the Threefold Lotus Sutra)

The Buddha introduces various events into our lives so that we can learn to revere all things. This is why we really do not have to worry, no matter what we encounter in life. It is all right to rejoice in peace, suffer in peace, and sorrow in peace. All we need to do is to train our eyes to see the light wherever it is shining in every such situation. When we can discern the light and revere all things, just being alive as we are will in itself be our path to buddhahood.

The Original Buddha exists in every part of the universe,

ready to [liberate] all beings of the universe. (*Buddhism for Today*, p. xxvi)

What is someone who can revere all things?

There once was a manager of a company. His company had been doing all right, but adverse business conditions led one of its main backers to withdraw its financial support, and the company found itself with considerable debts. The manager had been active in his Dharma center since his youth and had undergone religious training, but with his future now insecure, one day he said ironically to a leader of the center, "When times get rough, even our Rissho Kosei-kai teachings don't really help much, do they?"

Hearing this, the leader answered by asking him, "Are you sure you really think so? It seems to me that your problems are only in the present; what about up until now? How has life treated you so far?"

"What about up until now?" This question led the man back to rereading the founder's Dharma talks while looking into his own heart. He had to admit that his company had certainly been doing fine until recently. The company had had plenty of work and good times, and he recalled how he himself did his job earnestly and well and received support from a great many people.

He then thought about what the Buddha was trying to teach him through the medium of his present difficulties and what he was being called upon to do.

The reason I place so much emphasis on rejoicing is that, if only you will respect and live by the Buddha's teaching, you will without a doubt be happy. Therefore, when you put the teaching into practice with the joy of knowing there is nothing to worry about, you will experience a great sense of security. (*Hosshin* [Raising Aspirations], November 1986, p. 16)

The man was hoping from the bottom of his heart to pull him-self together. A feeling that he should in fact align himself with the wish of the Buddha filled his heart. After having given some thought to what the Buddha would wish for him, the following day he and his wife set out to visit the customers and others who had supported the company in the past and thank them for their help.

Wherever they went, people gave them at best only shallow words of sympathy or encouragement, saying, "Oh, yes, we heard about you; in big trouble, aren't you?" The couple had made up their minds to pay less attention to what others said, or how they might respond, and instead to simply do their best to venerate the buddha-nature of whomever they were with and try to establish a connection with them always through their own buddha-natures. The concrete form through which they expressed this determina-tion was to give thanks for the support they had received in the past.

And, if any work was offered, they determined to undertake it with wholehearted gratitude.

At this time they visited a certain company, where they were told, "Right now we have a lot of work we need to contract out, but we heard that your company was experiencing difficulties, so we were thinking of giving the contract to another company. How-ever, you have a very positive attitude—we're quite impressed," and with that they were offered a large contract. This turned out to be a watershed, and the man was subsequently quite successful in putting his company back on track.

Changes that arise from believing deeply in the Buddha Dharma and practicing it wholeheartedly attest that we are on the correct course. For example, something that seems on the surface to be a negative change may turn out to be a means to further hone our character. Therefore, we must go along with whatever happens, however disagreeable it may seem, and continue our practice of the Buddha Way, because then that unwanted change will become part of the foundation for our eventual happiness. (*Shinshaku Hokke Sambukyo* [New Commentary on the Threefold Lotus Sutra], vol. 4, p. 54)

When the company manager was about to turn sixty years old, the next situation he had to deal with involved his mother, who began to require daily care. "So, I guess this is another opportunity to find out how to realize the Buddha's wishes," he thought. After talking it over with his wife, he said, "I still have to do what I can to make myself useful to the company, but let's take this opportunity to perform our filial duties, something we haven't done much about so far." He resigned from his executive position with a fifty percent reduction in pay. His workload was cut by a third, and he now spends this time with his elderly mother. At present, the mother is the focus of the family, and the man and his wife are in spiritual accord and cooperate with each other better than they ever did before.

The man is no longer unduly influenced by the variously changing phenomena of the world and can see that the situations of having enough work, of not having enough work, and of caring for his mother are all stations along the path toward attaining buddhahood. By taking an approach that sees that "everything that happens is just what I need," he can carry on with a sense of what the Buddha expects of him in every situation, great or small.

As a caveat to the approach that "everything that happens is just what we need," we must keep in mind the great importance of relating to the people around us in a warmhearted way at all times if we want to truly connect with the Buddha's wishes. In other words, we need to ask ourselves if contact is happening between our own buddha-nature and the buddha-nature of others.

This is, in fact, what connects us with the Buddha's wishes. When we are connected with the Buddha's wishes, we gain the ability to see the light that is shining and thus live with great peace of mind.

The founder said, "You will be true to your self and sincerely follow the Buddha Way if you are honest and if you do not doubt yourself. That is the best way to ease your spirit. There is no greater peace than this." Peace of mind arises when you become aware of this, by abiding by the teaching of the Buddha that you received. The greatest peace of all arises with the realization that there is nothing to worry about because the Buddha is protecting you.

The Buddha's view is one of great warmth that adjusts itself to the understanding of the hearer. Learning to adopt this kind of view at all times is an exercise assigned to us by the Buddha. When we can see everything with the eyes of compassion in a way similar to the Buddha's, then we will be liberated and attain great peace of mind.

## 20 Seeing with the Eyes of Compassion
### Hoza *Sessions*

It has been said from long ago that the Sutras of Great Extent [Mahayana sutras] are the "masters of compassion." We really must make compassion the first order of business in our *hoza* sessions. When we display compassion, the problems raised in the sessions begin to be resolved, the session itself becomes of great interest, and all the steps discussed start to be put into practice.

—*Hosshin* (Raising Aspirations), August 1989

In the words of Founder Nikkyo Niwano, "We can all become happy if we look at things with compassionate eyes, as the Buddha did." How can we best put into practice what the founder has demonstrated for us—to see with compassionate eyes and open the way to liberation through *hoza* sessions? What does it mean to "make compassion the first order of business"?

The Buddha is the force that brings about liberation, but achieving this also depends on what we ourselves do. We are all granted countless opportunities to interact with others. Whether or not we can make our *hoza* sessions scenes of liberation depends on how we approach problems of another person and whether we can listen with empathy to the person's inner voice.

Without the gift of encounters with others, we cannot attain enlightenment and be happy by ourselves alone. *Hoza* sessions are a good place for us to learn this lesson from each other.

At one time, there was a married couple who had been living separate existences under the same roof for many years. Of all the problems raised at their Dharma center, this was one that everyone was united in the desire to solve. One after another, all kinds of ways and means were tried to get the couple to start talking to each other again, but somehow the situation never changed.

An opportunity later arose, however, for some of the members to ask the founder about the situation. His response was: "Do you realize how hard it must be for them to live in the same house year after year without ever speaking to each other? They must be making a strenuous effort to keep at this. You should be as nice as you can to them."

> Only when you naturally respect the individuality of others will your explanations of the Dharma sink into their hearts as the very words of the Buddha. (*Hosshin* [Raising Aspirations], April 1991, p. 17)

On hearing the words of the founder, the Dharma center leader did not at first understand, and her mind went blank. She did realize, however, that everything the center's members had been doing so far with all good intentions had been backfiring. They had made no attempt whatever to see the buddha-nature of the estranged husband and wife. All they had done was to keep preaching and trying to change the troubled couple for the better so that they could see the pair sharing their lives again.

Because we are all being given life in a context consisting of the working of the Buddha, in *hoza* sessions the truth reveals itself clearly before our eyes that "if I act this way, the person I am dealing with will act that way." Faith in the fact that we live in the Buddha's world and are being sustained in life by the Buddha begins with faith in just one other person. All we need is true faith in that one person. (*Hosshin* [Raising Aspirations], October 1987, p. 16)

We tend to concern ourselves particularly with the faults in other people and try to correct them. Even when we are faced with situations that look as if they are only causing difficulties, however, if we can discover even one positive aspect, it can open the way toward a solution. The ability to do this lies in the possession and daily application of a warm, compassionate attitude. With this ability, the problem itself then seems to our eyes as "a tiny window letting in a beam of light." In other words, we realize that it is an opportunity to discover buddha-nature in ourselves and others. As soon as we let ourselves flow out through that tiny window, we see a harmonious world in which all things are manifestations of buddha-nature. Our liberation starts to grow from the moment we see that harmonious world.

Rather than trying to eloquently preach the Dharma, I think it is better to talk to people so as to give them hope and expectations for a brighter future. I think we should do our best every day to say whatever we can to encourage people to feel that they are living worthwhile lives. (*Kosei,* August 1958, p. 10)

In time, the Dharma center leader paid a visit to the couple with a more thoughtful attitude and appreciation for the great effort they were making, hoping simply to offer to help in any way that she could. However, she found nobody at home. In fact, a short while before on that very day, the husband had suddenly fallen seriously ill. His wife called for an ambulance and went with him to the hospital.

After he recovered and was discharged from the hospital, they went together to the Dharma center to express their appreciation to the members. For the first time they spoke of their own accord to the others about the various problems that had led them to lead separate lives under the same roof.

> You should approach the person in front of you holding your hands in prayer and truly revering that person's spirit, with the feeling that "this person has been sent to me by the Buddha to teach me what I need to know piece by piece." When you do this, every person will tell you various true things about him- or herself without being asked. (*Hosshin* [Raising Aspirations], July 1991, p. 18)

What you need to learn from another person is not the cause of his or her suffering but how and why the person has managed to go on living and striving in the midst of that suffering. When you hear this, you will have heard that person's most precious tale and will thus be able to recognize and revere his or her buddha-nature. In the event that you can also enable that person to become conscious of his or her buddha-nature, true liberation will be the result.

The Buddha has given us a treasure that never dwindles even though we use it throughout our whole lives. We have already received many precious gifts from the Buddha during our lives so far. To feel truly happy, we need to be able to access that treasure even when we are troubled.

Trouble is not necessarily a bad situation—it can be an opportunity for our awakening. When you look with compassionate eyes at your own or someone else's suffering, you will see that it is bodhisattva practice and then even suffering becomes a basis for achieving happiness.

If we can approach the problems of others with compassionate eyes, as the founder did, and see the precious opportunities within those problems, the discussions we have of difficulties in *hoza* sessions will never deteriorate into mere gossip. In fact, such discussions will then become truly helpful and charitable, bringing happiness to all. This kind of *hoza* session allows everyone to speak freely and becomes an opportunity for the Dharma to come alive.

*Hoza* sessions are the lifeblood of Rissho Kosei-kai. They form the core of our practice of faith. (*Niwano Nikkyo Jiden* [Nikkyo Niwano, an Autobiography], p. 189)

Without the ability to perceive the happiness of the present moment, an ambitious spirit that sees what is lacking and strives for improvement will find in its ambition the seeds of anxiety and suffering. People who are happy are people who are skillful at finding true joy. When you seek what you can be grateful for, you will live a rich life; but when you concentrate on what you lack, you enter the path of pain and suffering.

"We should not always speak of and look at the bad sides to one's character. We should look with thoughtful regard at what a person is striving for and what he or she is suffering." When I think of the founder, who spoke these words, I am reminded of the kindness with which he always regarded others.

Unless our own hearts are warm and pure like the Buddha's,

we cannot guide others to liberation. That is the point to remember. (*San Raizan Meiso* [Meditations from Three Holy Mountains], p. 86)

## 21 Recognizing Buddha-Nature
### *Reflection*

The most deeply fundamental reflection arises from a keenly felt recollection of the fact that we are being sustained in life by the Buddha. This recollection leads us to reevaluate what we have done and reflect, "I am being sustained in life by the Buddha, but have my actions been consistent with this fact?"

—*Niwano Nikkyo Howa Senshu*
(Selected Dharma Talks of Nikkyo Niwano)

Founder Nikkyo Niwano said, "Nothing is more precious than sincere reflection. People who can sincerely reflect and correct soon find liberation."

Reflection does not mean simply looking back on your past actions and feeling regret; it means reflecting on the fact that you were unable to see reality as it is, thus failing to perceive what the Buddha was expecting from you at the time. This is what reflection means for people on the Buddhist path.

With true reflection, the real reason a problem occurred

becomes apparent. The real reason is not the cause of the problem but rather the purpose of the problem.

> Here we are clearly told that the highest form of reflection is to perceive things as they really are—to realize the ultimate reality of all things. (*Shinshaku Hokke Sambu-kyo* [New Commentary on the Threefold Lotus Sutra], vol. 10, p. 172)

When we are unable to draw close to the Buddha is when we are seeing things in simple terms of black and white or right and wrong. It is important for us to seek greater happiness and try to avoid making the same mistakes over and over again.

However, the world of the Lotus Sutra is not one in which we see things in terms of right and wrong and try to change what we perceive as evil in ourselves. When we can realize the Buddha's wish that transcends questions of right and wrong, our spirits are released from suffering and we awaken to the feeling: "Oh, so that is it! This is the purpose for which I am living." With that realization, where we are living, in the here and now, is transformed into the world of the Lotus Sutra, a world that is like the blossom in the sutra's title, growing out of the muddy water and bursting into bloom.

> Reflection in Buddhism involves strict and constant scrutiny of the preciousness of your true nature as well as of your actual imperfections. (*Niwano Nikkyo Howa Senshu* [Selected Dharma Talks of Nikkyo Niwano], special volume, p. 156)

I once knew of a young woman whose general health was so poor that she often had to go to the hospital to receive an intravenous drip. Unfortunately, her veins were too small in diameter to easily accommodate the needle. The physician always had to search for a suitable blood vessel and try several times before he was able to insert the needle successfully. This was a painful process, and the young woman soon felt angry at the doctor every time she had to receive the treatment.

One day when she was attending a Rissho Kosei-kai meeting, she burst out with an angry remark about her situation, asking, "Does my doctor always have to put me through this pain? He must not be a very good doctor; isn't there another one who could do a better job?"

Learning of this outburst, the founder met her and said, "Your physician is also having a hard time every time he gives you the intravenous treatment. Don't you think you are lucky to have a doctor who is willing to go to that much trouble for you? If putting the blame on him could help to cure you, that would be a good thing. But that is not what faith teaches us."

The young woman caught her breath. She realized in her heart that she had been displaying the wrong attitude, because she understood that her sessions at the hospital also had the purpose of teaching her how to venerate all people. After this realization, she was always gracious and spoke politely to her doctor while he was treating her.

The founder's words enabled her to reflect and correct, and so her displeasure could turn into gratitude. She then became able to recognize her situation as advantageous and could be happy.

The more often we turn our gaze toward the precious gifts we are receiving, the more joy we feel, and we are thus able to live happier and richer lives. To reflect means to recognize in what spirit we should be leading our lives. This involves our realization that we should be communicating with words that originate from our buddha-nature. That is why it is said that "reflection is joy."

When our hearts reflect and correct and we feel purified, our hearts become responsive to the heart of the Buddha in an instant. (Speech at Fumon Hall, Tokyo, September 23, 1973)

What the Buddha wishes for us is that we realize our buddha-nature. We reflect and correct not in order to solve our problems but to recognize our own buddha-nature. When we do so and our point of view shifts to that of the Buddha, which sees the world of liberation, we realize that our suffering occurs in order to lead us along the path to the attainment of buddhahood. For that we can rejoice.

Because the problems we face are in fact placed on our path to liberation by the Buddha, when we realize this we can begin to overcome those problems. When we recognize the Buddha's wish and open ourselves to our own buddha-nature, bad situations have a way of reversing themselves, and our problems begin to disappear. Reflection as described and taught in the Lotus Sutra equals the attainment of buddhahood by ourselves together with others.

## 22 Recognizing the Source of Our Existence
### *Ancestor Appreciation*

Appreciating one's ancestors is recognizing the source of one's existence. It is knowing the roots of one's life. Ancestor appreciation begins with our becoming aware of how blessedly they support us.
—*Yakushin* (Progress), April 1979

Founder Nikkyo Niwano often said, "What we teach in Rissho Kosei-kai are ancestor appreciation and filial piety." We are blessed with innumerable ancestors, and it is because their lives have been connected without interruption that each of us exists in the here and now. Our ancestors are the source of our own existence, making it possible for us to live. Giving form to the warmness of heart that wells up when we sense the emotions that were surely felt by our ancestors, who are the sources of our own lives—that is ancestor appreciation.

If you look for the source of the suffering that may be confronting you now, you are likely to interpret it as arising because you have troubled ancestors. If you think that the reason you recite the sutra is to purify the spirits of the troubled ancestors whose suffering has become an obstacle to your happiness, their lives will be unrewarded.

A life that experienced untold suffering is also a life that has been lived to the fullest. One concept in the Lotus Sutra is the showing of consideration for and respect to one's ancestors with the understanding that they underwent considerable suffering so that one could exist now.

When we feel a warmhearted bond with our ancestors and look upon them kindly, that will certainly enable us to see the buddha-nature in the lives that all of them led, whereupon our understanding of the lives of our ancestors changes and a feeling of gratitude wells up in us. Then we understand the value of our own lives, our existence and aspirations having been inherited from them, and from that the lives of their descendants begin to change.

> It goes without saying that it is thanks to our ancestors that we exist now in this world. If, for the sake of argument, we envision this concept as a tree, then our ancestors are the tree's roots; we, their descendants, are the branches and leaves; and our parents are the trunk. The roots need to be nourished first for the branches and leaves to grow strong and healthy and then for blossoms and seeds to develop. It is only by understanding this process that we can receive the blessings of nature. It is in accord with the path for all human beings. (*Niwano Nikkyo Howa Senshu* [Selected Dharma Talks of Nikkyo Niwano], vol. 4, p. 248)

There once was a woman, the youngest of six children, who lost her parents when she was quite young and was reared by an older sister. First the sister who took care of her, and then her other siblings, each fell ill and passed away, one by one, leaving her all alone. As she was also frail, she was slow to recover from colds and suffered from severe headaches. Whenever she would fall ill, she would worry from the thought that, like her parents and siblings, her destiny might also be to die young. On one occasion, she shared this worry with the founder, and the founder replied in the following way.

"You should not worry. Your parents and siblings have all entrusted their hopes to you and have left you to lead your own life. They are all protecting you, so you are going to be all right. You will live a long and healthy life."

The woman was greatly relieved when she heard this. The unease in the back of her mind departed, and in its place were warm thoughts of her parents and brothers and sister. A feeling of gratitude toward those who had already passed away welled up inside her, and from that point on she was able to recite the sutra with a sense of wholehearted gratitude to them. Amazingly, after that she never fell ill again.

> Rather than praying to the spirits of our ancestors in fear of some sort of punishment or curse, we should honor the virtues of our ancestors with a feeling of gratitude and pledge to strive to become a person about whom they could have peace of mind. That attitude should be our mainstay. And that is the starting point of ancestor appreciation. (*Niwano Nikkyo Howa Senshu* [Selected Dharma Talks of Nikkyo Niwano], vol. 4, p. 248)

In fact, our attitude toward our ancestors should be the same as our attitude toward the living. If we take the viewpoint of the principle that bad causes lead to bad effects, thinking that we as descendants suffer some misfortune because our ancestors incurred someone's enmity, we will find no relief, since we cannot change the lives of our ancestors. If we were correct in that viewpoint, there would be no meaning to having devotional faith.

Searching for the cause of affliction or suffering results in the denial of the lives our ancestors or we ourselves have lived. We learn about the past to clearly recognize the present merits or liberation we have acquired. In order to discover the working of the Buddha in our lives, we must learn from the lives of our ancestors. By becoming aware of what they must have felt, we can realize our present liberation.

> In order to attain enlightenment, in order to find happiness, we must worship in such a way as to purify our minds and hearts, starting by paying respect to our roots. (*Hosshin* [Raising Aspirations], August 1986, p. 16)

Just as we cannot change our past, we cannot erase the lives of our ancestors. If we, as descendants of our ancestors, can look upon them warmheartedly regardless of what their lives may have been like, and if we can use this as an opportunity to manifest kindness of heart and lead an even better life, it is thanks to them. If we as their descendants think in this way, they should be greatly pleased.

As the idea of dependent origination—the basic foundation of the Lotus Sutra—teaches us, all the events that occur in our lives serve as factors in our spiritual liberation when we accept them as conditions that help us open the buddha-nature within ourselves. Even everything that happened in our past, which we are not able to change, can be considered a precious treasure. And isn't that the preciousness of the Lotus Sutra that the founder taught us about?

## 23 Demonstrating a Buddha-Heart
### *Dissemination Work*

We often talk about one of our activities—the "general guidance movement"—in which members visit other members' homes in a specific area to invite them to attend activities at a Dharma center. This activity is a call to everyone to reveal their buddha-nature together.

—*Niwano Nikkyo Howa Senshu*
(Selected Dharma Talks of Nikkyo Niwano)

Founder Nikkyo Niwano often said, "Rissho Kosei-kai is an organization dedicated to sharing the essence of the Lotus Sutra."

The Lotus Sutra contains a variety of parables, but nowhere among them are stories in which the Buddha forces the teaching, like good medicine, down his followers' throats or scolds them for not taking it. The Buddha always trusts us, waits for us with infinite patience, gives us what we wish for, pleases us, and calms our fears as he leads us along the path.

Carrying out exactly what the Lotus Sutra teaches—that is what it means to share the essence of the Lotus Sutra.

Rather than think of ourselves as representatives of the Buddha teaching others, we should think of ourselves as helping the Buddha to teach others. Like Punna-Mantaniputta, known for his skill in communicating the Dharma to other people, the praiseworthy among us are those who can spread the Dharma and put it into practice. (*Niwano Nikkyo Howa Senshu* [Selected Dharma Talks of Nikkyo Niwano], vol. 4, p. 275)

Leading others to the faith is a way of establishing warm, friendly relations with other people. These activities also serve to create "seeds for growth" by helping us reconfirm our own feelings of gratitude and liberation.

The important points in this regard are to feel empathy for the anxiety, suffering, and joy of other people, and discover the virtue and effort in their situation, and then place your hands together in reverence and learn what you can from that situation. An indispensable part of this process is to express in words your wishes for other people's happiness and your perception of their buddha-nature.

The only art to guiding others lies in the heartfelt wish for the other person's happiness. Everything else proceeds from this. (*Niwano Nikkyo Howa Senshu* [Selected Dharma Talks of Nikkyo Niwano], special volume, p. 177)

I once had an opportunity to talk with the leader of the young housewives' group at a certain Dharma center, who told me about her situation. A local woman she had persuaded to join the group often contacted her just before events to which she had been invited to say, "My son has suddenly developed a fever—I won't be able to come in today." The leader of the group always felt extremely disappointed by this and thought to herself, "I wish she had come in and performed her duties; in doing that the fact of her son's illness would have helped open up the world of divine protection to her." At the same time, however, she was unsure whether this was the right way to pursue the relationship.

I told her, "Why don't you try to put the woman at ease and treat her with respect, saying, 'You seem to be very kind—your son is lucky to have such a good mother. I am sure it isn't easy for you, but go ahead and take good care of your son. Just let me know if there is anything I can do to help.' If it were me, I would much rather hear something like that than 'Why aren't you coming?' If you speak to her kindly and she gets the idea that you sincerely would like to see her at events, I'm sure she will show up one day soon."

> For people leading ordinary lives like us, it is impossible to completely eradicate all worldly desires. We have to find peace of mind "without cutting off [our] earthly cares and renouncing [our] five desires," as the Sutra of Meditation on the Bodhisattva Universal Virtue says. (*Yakushin* [Progress], February 1974, p. 10)

If you try to force the Dharma on someone, saying, "This is how it ought to be" or "This is a good thing," somewhere along the line you will reach an impasse and start to feel regretful. The Dharma does not exist to be applied to people; it exists to help them achieve happiness.

The true "world of divine protection" consists in the discovery of both liberation and joy within the events and encounters we are experiencing here and now. We need to feel this and catch hold of it.

Without getting too concerned about the reality that things do not always work out as you would like, look to discover and draw out the buddha-nature in others by developing a warm, caring spirit. It is not your words that communicate with others. It is your spirit that, with the warmth that develops and grows, reaches out to them.

> If one has the opportunity to come into contact with a teaching that provides real peace of mind and deep satisfaction, one will gladly accept it. (*Shinshaku Hokke Sambu-kyo* [New Commentary on the Threefold Lotus Sutra], vol. 7, p. 141)

However, worries such as those of the leader of the young housewives' group occurred precisely because she came into contact with many people and felt warm and sympathetic toward them. Feeling great appreciation for such a sincere young woman, I told her, "You are really exercising your spirit on behalf of others, and that is a wonderful thing. I hope you will accept with joy the fact that you are able to demonstrate your kindness through your relations with others in this way."

Hearing this, her face brightened, and she replied, "When I accept that I am able to be demonstrating warmth, I can also be more accepting of others. When I am able to do this, I will be able to embrace others with warmth regularly."

> A conversation with someone or hearing someone talking about his or her problem can serve as an opportunity to plant a seed that will spring into life and grow into enlightenment. It is said that "buddha-seeds spring from causation." I believe that the seeds of buddhahood are indeed awakened through causation. (*Hosshin* [Raising Aspirations], January 1992, p. 17)

The existence of others gives us the opportunity to share the teachings and demonstrate our own warmth while making contact with them. People do not exist for the sake of the teachings; the teachings exist for people, in order to bring them joy.

Thus, rather than immediately trying to teach others, first show how happy you are for being able to perform guidance work. Just try to communicate your own joyful feelings and warm spirit. You do not have to push yourself hard. You will discover your own buddha-nature as well as that of others and feel spiritual warmth during the natural course of your relationship. When you feel your own spirit warming, you will start to look forward to your next meeting.

As you continue to wish for the happiness of others and work to lead them to the faith, in time you will find that you have also developed and grown closer to the Buddha. As is written in chapter 20 of the Lotus Sutra, "The Bodhisattva Never Despise," "Because under former buddhas . . . I preached it [this sutra] to others, I soon attained Perfect Enlightenment." That is, by teaching others we ourselves become buddhas.

> We must make ourselves a "good condition" for all persons and nurture faith in them. This is the shortest way, and also the true way, to guide other people. (*Shinshaku Hokke Sambu-kyo* [New Commentary on the Threefold Lotus Sutra], vol. 4, p. 65)

Founder Niwano once said to members, "We ask every one of you to give guidance to at least one other person because the process of relating to that other person while sincerely hoping for his or her happiness functions as a devotional exercise for your own benefit."

In pursuing dissemination work, the problems being borne by others serve as lessons to us and help us to grow and embark on our true path in life. Rather than simply seek to reform the other person, when you focus your mind on how the Buddha cares about others, your own spirit gradually comes closer to this ideal. The Buddha will reward you with an outcome that corresponds to the progress of your spirit. Our dissemination work is all about savoring this process.

> We must never lose sight of the ultimate purpose, which is to lead others eventually to the truth about the world and human beings that the Buddha has taught us. (*Shinshaku Hokke Sambu-kyo* [New Commentary on the Threefold Lotus Sutra], vol. 4, p. 66)

We are "the Buddha's messengers." The role of the Buddha's messengers is to revere the buddha-nature of all people. To create an atmosphere in which anyone can speak confidently, first of all we need to rid ourselves of our preconceptions and listen carefully to what others have to say, without preparing our reply in advance.

Doing this helps us to adopt a warm-hearted attitude and think of those who are experiencing hardships as "people making strenuous efforts" and people who are shouldering irksome responsibilities as "bodhisattvas giving their all to others." Such an attitude also transforms people who seem selfish and self-centered into "people who can express themselves just as they are."

> All people possess buddha-nature, or more precisely, all people originally are buddha-nature itself. No matter how you consider this, it is an incontrovertible truth. (*Niwano Nikkyo*

*Howa Senshu* [Selected Dharma Talks of Nikkyo Niwano], special volume, p. 56)

Even though you believe you are doing it for other people's own good, when your approach is one of attempting to reform their faults, they will never open their hearts to you. It is best initially to praise their virtues.

The human heart is honest. When treated warmly, people will respond with warmth, and when they feel accepted, they will feel secure and forget their suffering. Then the strength to make a new start and move ahead will come into play.

There is no more virtuous deed than guiding others. Guiding others creates more buddhas in this world. (*Niwano Nikkyo Howa Senshu* [Selected Dharma Talks of Nikkyo Niwano], special volume, p. 270)

The founder taught us, "There is no greater virtue than to sow seeds of encounter with the Buddha."

As a result of our dissemination work, it is a fact that people have come into contact with the Dharma and found happiness. I hope we can continue to do that with pride.

## 24 Becoming a Buddha Each Day
### Buddhism in Everyday Life

In the final analysis, Buddhism is daily life. It teaches us as living human beings how to be and how to live.

—*Niwano Nikkyo Howa Senshu*
(Selected Dharma Talks of Nikkyo Niwano)

Founder Nikkyo Niwano has taught us, "Wherever you may be, make use of a worldview shaped by the Lotus Sutra. That is, create warm, friendly contacts. If you strive to do this, you will become someone with a radiant aura, like the Buddha."

I have four children. When I have to say good-bye to my children to go to my office, they sometimes cry and beg me not to leave. Nothing saddens a mother more than to make her children feel lonely. One feels sorry for them and wonders why it is necessary to make them unhappy.

Still, when this kind of uproar comes to be repeated every day, one begins to feel a little annoyed on one's own behalf and thinks, "Really, they never listen to what they are told! This is becoming tiresome."

However, if we try to catch a glimpse of the working of the Buddha even in this kind of dealing with our children in the course of daily life, I think we can do so.

When my children say, "Don't go," I look beyond their words to the feeling in their hearts that says, "I love you, Mommy." Each of the four is unique—some cry, some get angry, but when I consider these emotions as expressions of love, I feel truly glad and they seem lovable to me.

Then I can answer them with a heart warmed by these feelings and say, "Mommy loves you, too. I wonder why I have to go out today. I am going to feel lonesome, too." In other words, I make clear to them my feelings of love for each of them.

That's all there is to it, but when I first began doing this, I realized that something seemed to make my relationship to my children warmer. While still crying, they would wave good-bye to me and tell me to have a good day. This moment of contact with, well, in actual fact departure from, my children has now become important and precious to me.

Perhaps *shojin,* one of the Six Perfections, means "bringing into play the same feelings that the Buddha would have" in every moment of every day.

> Buddhism is not something you follow by renouncing the world or practice in the intervals when you are not pursuing worldly matters. Buddhism amounts to how you live, twenty-four hours a day, and how you accept and apply the Buddha's teachings as the mainstay of your life. (*Niwano Nikkyo Howa Senshu* [Selected Dharma Talks of Nikkyo Niwano], special volume, p. 189)

When I recall the founder and what he was like, it occurs to me that "buddha-nature" is not just a demonstration of one's virtues.

I have the feeling that it is, in fact, something more warm and friendly than that.

What the Buddha is asking of us is that we should consistently increase our efforts to discover the warmth that lies behind the words and actions of others and to speak to others with such warmth. Probably that is all there is to it.

By repeatedly having this type of warm and friendly contact with others, we can someday become buddhas. At the same time, in those everyday small contacts, we become buddhas completely even if just for a moment. I believe that this is what bodhisattva practice by lay Buddhists means. Every day, we become buddhas.

> When you are giving yourself to the service of others, during that time you forget yourself and attain buddhahood. (*Niwano Nikkyo Howa Senshu* [Selected Dharma Talks of Nikkyo Niwano], special volume, p. 72)

In the course of our daily lives, we express by the way we live our awareness that we, and others as well, are endowed with the buddha-nature that radiates brilliantly in us. That is the essence of how lay followers of Buddhism should lead their lives. We are bodhisattvas who act in the awareness that we live in order to become buddhas.

## 25 When You Change Yourself
### *Three Thousand Realms in a Single Thought*

When your way of thinking is firmly in conformity with the heart of the Buddha, that moment of pure, heartfelt wishing for the happiness of others that you experience communicates itself to anyone you are with, and this is repeated in turn to another and yet still another person. Thus the circle of happiness grows, and of course you will also harvest the fruit of approaching buddhahood.
—*San Reizan Meiso* (Meditations from Three Holy Mountains)

Founder Nikkyo Niwano taught us that "if you want to be happy, you must first change yourself." His words refer not just to changing something in our behavior or other more obvious characteristics; first and foremost they refer to drawing ourselves nearer to "the outlook of the Buddha who sees the joy in the here and now as things are."

We are ordained to live in a world of dependent origination, which is a world of transience where everything must and does change. Because we have been given life in a world of dependent origination, when we affirm the now and perceive its merit, anything that happened in the past is seen to have had a good cause, and accordingly, whatever is to come in the future will bring good results.

> Various events are constantly occurring all around us. In our interpersonal relations as well, a variety of people are involved, including those with whom we get along and those with whom we do not get along. Even if you try, it is not possible to have your own way in all of your relationships with people and events. You must first correctly adjust your own mind, and when you achieve that, the ideas and actions of the people you are involved with fall into place in accordance with that single thought of yours. (*San Reizan Meiso* [Meditations from Three Holy Mountains], p. 80)

When you regard others, and yourself as well, rather than trying to immediately bring about change, you should try to see all as the buddha-nature itself and try to realize that dealing with suffering is part of the active effort people make. When you see what is wrong and try to correct it or change it, even though you may be doing your best with a warm and affectionate spirit, things will often not progress as you wish, and both you and the other person may end up having a difficult and unpleasant time.

The husband of a certain Rissho Kosei-kai Dharma center leader was set against her activities and constantly told her, "Your so-called faith is nothing but complacent self-satisfaction." She sought guidance from the founder, and he gave her the following answer: "Well, your husband was actually extolling you! A faith that satisfies you is the greatest happiness you can achieve, isn't it? You should understand what he says as praise and be grateful to him."

Religion is in fact what allows your spirit to receive true joy, what opens your mind, sets it free from all fetters, and gives rise to feelings of gratitude for the unlimited gifts bestowed by the great natural world. This is truly the benefit of religion, and as extra bonuses, the satisfactions of your life become abundant and things start to go well for you. (*Niwano Nikkyo Howa Senshu* [Selected Dharma Talks of Nikkyo Niwano], special volume, p. 121)

It is not surprising that the center leader felt sad and distressed when her husband said that her faith was just selfish, self-satisfied complacency. Somewhere in the back of her mind, however, she had been thinking, "Thanks to my faith, our home is a happy place," and that if anyone needed to change, it was her husband, not herself. By assuming that she was the one that deserved appreciation, she could not determine how she should change and found herself at a loss.

At this point, the founder surprised her by telling her that her husband was singing her praises and she should be grateful to him. The foundation of faith is a joyful heart. Because the founder knew this better than anyone, he was regularly able to take joy in everything. When one's spirit feels joy, that sense of happiness is communicated in a widening circle around one.

When we are laboring as bodhisattvas for the sake of others, how much joy does that give us? Are we really aware of our faith's true value and how fortunate we are to have it?

What the founder was teaching us was that when the center leader's husband called her faith activities self-satisfying, rather than take his words as criticism, she should understand them as welcome evidence of the faith that was giving her joy, and with her joyful heart draw closer to her husband. The ability to do this, he was saying, is part of the true value of religious faith.

The Buddha always defends us with his great compassion and mercy. He also gives trials that are sometimes difficult to overcome to people who are capable of advanced religious training, instead of leaving them only in easy and favorable situations. Overcoming such difficulties leads us to truly recognize the Buddha's immense parental benevolence and realize that we indeed are children of the Buddha. This allows us to attain a genuinely joyful state of mind. (*Hosshin* [Raising Aspirations], February 1992, p. 17)

This world we are living in is an impermanent one of ceaseless change. The way to influence change in this ever-changing world is a matter of using our own hearts and nothing else.

An impermanent world can be one of hope, in which we can continue to learn and progress throughout our lives. If we can change our own hearts and minds so that we can perceive our buddha-nature and adopt a joyful outlook, even relationships that have so far seemed confrontational can become cordial on both sides, and a world radiant with the light of buddha-nature opens up before us.

The founder was well acquainted with true joy, and his insights have so far brought liberation to countless people. He has shown us how the world can become better through the insights of just one person who realizes true joy.

It might not be easy for us to acquire such insights as the founder showed. Even so, however, we can hear the voice of another person's buddha-nature loud and clear if we can pick up clues and understand from their words and actions what is bothering them. If we can do that and speak to the other person with warmth and empathy, it will constitute a full-fledged expression of our own present joy and a crystallization of compassion and wisdom.

When we relate to people with the sincere wish that they will somehow realize how happy they are, they can develop of their own accord the ability to improve themselves.

> In a single thought in your own mind, three thousand realms come into view. That is Three Thousand Realms in a Single Thought. If you think in the right way and you come under the divine guidance and protection of the gods and the buddhas, you become able to enjoy life together with all the members of your family. My household is an extremely lively one. When I leave the house in the morning and when I come home in the evening, my four grandchildren, starting with the seven-year-old, gather around me. When I exclaim, "Here come those youngsters again!" or words like that, there's a great to-do. When the grandchildren are around me, I never stop laughing. (*Niwano Nikkyo Howa Senshu* [Selected Dharma Talks of Nikkyo Niwano], vol. 4, p. 89)

## 26 Families That Raise Bodhisattvas
### *Affectionate, United Families*

Every person has something wonderful deep down inside him- or herself. The important thing is to draw that out.
*—Niwano Nikkyo Howa Senshu*
(Selected Dharma Talks of Nikkyo Niwano)

My grandfather, Founder Nikkyo Niwano, used to call each of his grandchildren "mini-bodhisattva": thinking of that, I can again hear his warm voice and see his smile in my mind.

At that time we were still too young to understand what our grandfather really meant when he called us mini-bodhisattvas, but we could tell from his kind expression and warm tone of voice that it was something very special, and so we grew up believing we were that very wonderful thing.

"You cannot bring about a change of heart in another person simply by telling him he should feel a certain way or should open his mind. You can only do this when you are able to become a person who awakens a mind like the Buddha's in the other person," my grandfather said. In keeping with these words, he consistently interacted with us in such a way as to bring about such an awakening.

By calling me a mini-bodhisattva, he awakened in me the desire to become a bodhisattva.

True education is never forced. It is a drawing-out process in which the qualities that fit each individual are drawn out and developed, while a humanitarian spirit is nurtured in all. (*Kosei,* April 1977, p. 15)

One time when I was still in high school, I went out with a friend and ended up staying out much later than I had intended. Because I rushed back without calling home along the way, I was sure my parents would be upset and worrying about me. I had my excuses ready, however, and arrived home going over in my mind what I would say to any scolding I received.

When I entered the living room, contrary to my expectations, the only person present was my grandfather, who was watching television. The hour was long past the time he usually retired to his own room, where he had a television of his own. Wondering what was going on, I simply said, "I'm home." "Ah, there you are. Good. Now I feel much more at ease, thank you. I'll be going off to bed now," he replied, turning off the TV and standing up. "Good night, then," he said, and went to his room. This was all over in just a few moments, and I found myself standing there thinking, "What was that all about?"

My grandfather had thanked me for making him feel at ease, but I had not particularly intended to do anything to make him feel at ease or for which to be thanked. In fact, he had been worrying about me and was sitting up alone awaiting my return.

He didn't say anything like "I've been worried about you" or "Weren't you supposed to come home earlier?" From that time, however, I decided from the bottom of my heart that I would never, ever again do anything to cause my grandfather to worry about me.

> To create a home in which all your family members can attain buddhahood, you can take advantage of the doctrine of the Three Thousand Realms in a Single Thought. When you speak to members of your family with the sincerity that arises from your buddha-nature, everyone will begin speaking to one another in a spirit of sincerity, and your family will grow into one that can truly communicate. (*Hosshin* [Raising Aspirations], August 1987, p. 17)

Once I was really surprised when someone asked me, "What kind of guidance did you receive from the founder at home?" The founder did not give us any particular "guidance" at home. To us he was simply our kind and beloved grandfather.

Whenever he was with us, just the warmth of our being together made us feel at ease and secure because we sensed that he always thought of us as good and considered us as precious to him. He educated us by nurturing our desire to respond to his feelings about us. That is how he put us on the Path of the One Vehicle, the path that leads all to buddhahood.

> At first glance, you may fail to see the merit in doing for others or for society and so on, but when you pitch in and give it your best, you will find people starting to join you. Members of your family will draw closer to you. Your grandchildren will come to you. Your home will become a restful refuge. (*Niwano Nikkyo Howa Senshu* [Selected Dharma Talks of Nikkyo Niwano], vol. 4, p. 89)

## 27 Like the Light of the Sun and the Moon
### *The Founder*

People who are strong in their faith take on a different air. They become cheerful and full of confidence, with a positive and unflaggingly attentive approach to everything. These qualities become apparent of their own accord in their expression, speech, and action.

—*Niwano Nikkyo Howa Senshu*
(Selected Dharma Talks of Nikkyo Niwano)

One time, a Buddhist priest came to visit Rissho Kosei-kai headquarters in Tokyo, and in speaking to officers of the organization, he said, "Every day you see people placing their hands together in reverence to Founder Niwano and calling him teacher. You should not think of him only as you see him now. Think of how many difficulties he experienced before everyone began to revere him in this way! If you lose sight of all that he went through, you might not find your own liberation."

When you look back at the history of both the organization and the life of the founder, you can readily see that the founder often did not walk an easy road. Quite the contrary, as if it were the way he chose for himself, he faced many difficulties and repeatedly had to persevere in trying circumstances. The founder, however, perceived this rough road as the will of the gods and the buddhas, and with the spirit of the One Buddha-Vehicle, or the One Vehicle, he saw the difficulties as his reason for living and as work worth doing, and he made his way with joy and magnanimity.

A person who sincerely believes shines with light that is like a halo. That is the kind of person I would like to be. (*San Reizan Meiso* [Meditations from Three Holy Mountains], p. 145)

In daytime the sun lights up the world and nurtures living things, and in the dark of night the light of the moon relieves us of our daily cares and helps to illuminate our footsteps along the path of life. The most common Japanese kanji character for *brightness* is a composite of the characters for *sun* and *moon,* reminding me of the founder. He had a full understanding of our weaknesses and, in times of both joy and sorrow, always shed his radiance on us with a warm and loving countenance.

The founder always took the lead in showing us that the light of the One Vehicle was the most perfect light. He never stopped giving us the courage and hope we needed to live.

I happen to be the type who does not mind trouble and have always been an optimist. I left my mountain village home in Niigata Prefecture to come to Tokyo when I was seventeen years old, and at that time my father sent me off with the following farewell, "If you want to establish yourself in the world, you should choose the most bone-breaking job with the longest hours and lowest pay you can find." . . . I always kept those words of my father's deep in my heart, even as I took on my work in interreligious cooperation and efforts such as the World Conference of Religions for Peace. (*Niwano Nikkyo Howa Senshu* [Selected Dharma Talks of Nikkyo Niwano], vol. 4, p. 93)

The founder often used to talk to me about his youth. I loved hearing these stories from the time I was little, because his conversation was always about things that were amusing or pleasant.

About being raised in a poor mountain village far from the capital, the founder said, "That was a matter of greatest blessing for me." With regard to his experience of having to help out at home from when he was a small child and about being the second son (who was not able to inherit the family property in pre–World War II Japan), as well as about coming to Tokyo to work and almost immediately experiencing the Great Kanto Earthquake of 1923, his time in the military, and his days making Japanese pickles and selling them door-to-door, the founder always said, "That was actually all really worthwhile—I am truly grateful for those experiences." I never became bored listening to his stories no matter how many times I heard them, and he kept me on the edge of my seat until the end even when I knew what was going to happen next.

Your life is going to be your life, so you might as well live it with gratitude and joy; you will be happier, your surroundings will become brighter, and you will be one more reason for the world's becoming a more peaceful place. (*Kosei,* July 1968, p. 11)

During his time in the Japanese navy, the founder saw that many officers struck the men of lower ranks as a matter of course. Believing that people are naturally good and that nobody needs to be slapped to get the point of something, he never once used violence on those below him, and he even took superior officers' blows in place of the lower-ranking men before everyone's eyes.

I am truly blessed no matter where I go. In the military as well, though everyone complained about how hard things were, my three years in the navy was the time in my life when I was most able to act as I wished in performing tasks assigned to me; I think of it as a positive time for me. (*Niwano Nikkyo Howa Senshu* [Selected Dharma Talks of Nikkyo Niwano], vol. 4, p. 68)

Around 1955, the public was becoming wary of the explosive postwar growth of new religions and religious groups, and the *Yomiuri Shimbun,* Japan's largest-circulation newspaper, mounted a campaign critical of some Rissho Kosei-kai activities. The persistent criticism had its effect, and the founder was called to testify before the Judicial Affairs Committee of the House of Representatives of the Japanese Diet.

Every word the founder said at that time was carefully taken down and preserved. When I later read these reports and understood how the founder faced even that ordeal with such great dignity, I could only feel proud to be a member of Rissho Kosei-kai.

Among his statements were these words: "This occasion must be taken by all of our members, myself included, as an opportunity to return to the basics of our religious training and liberation through the Lotus Sutra." He even expressed thanks for this so-called Yomiuri Incident, and called the *Yomiuri Shimbun,* which started the whole affair, Yomiuri Bodhisattva, giving the newspaper company his gratitude for what he endured and learned.

> Because I hold the Buddha securely in my heart, I am not shaken by whatever occurs. (*Niwano Nikkyo Howa Senshu* [Selected Dharma Talks of Nikkyo Niwano], vol. 4, p. 231)

In the course of his ninety-three years of life, the founder accomplished and bequeathed to us so many impressive achievements that we cannot even begin to appreciate them all. Among these, the one for which we should be most grateful is that for those of us who were able to meet him, we became able to understand the things in life that in fact have true value.

> When I realized that the Lotus Sutra was the source through which every single being that has been given life can find liberation, I thought, "This is what I have been seeking," and determined that I should bring the teachings of the Lotus Sutra to as many people as possible. (*Niwano Nikkyo Howa Senshu* [Selected Dharma Talks of Nikkyo Niwano], vol. 4, p. 137)

The founder changed our feelings of anxiety into peace and joy, and our mistakes and hard times into opportunities, and he transformed the pains and sorrows of life into the Buddha's blessings. With the light of a faith that never lost its intensity, he showed us the bright hope of lasting peace, leading us to walk together with him on the Path of the One Vehicle.

> My prayer is simply to be allowed to carry out my mission. (*Tada Hitasurani* [Only Single-Mindedly], p. 32)

## 28 Encounters Are Everything
### *Cultivating the Fields in Our Hearts and Minds*

The Lotus Sutra is all about encounters, and it tells us to treasure every one. The concept of "causes and conditions" is also all about encounters. The Buddha's wish for us is that we make our encounters and meetings with other people into wonderful events.

—*Tada Hitasurani* (Only Single-Mindedly)

Founder Nikkyo Niwano told us, "Encounters are everything. They all stem from dependent origination." He also said, "What we call *en,* or encounters, is truthfully of extreme importance."

During a business trip in Japan when the founder was on one of the nation's high-speed Shinkansen trains, he went to the restroom and did not return to his seat for rather a long time. His secretary became worried, and when the founder did return, he asked if he was all right. The founder replied, "It was kind of untidy in there, so I was just cleaning it up a bit."

This was not a case of his moralistically cleaning the dirty restroom. We only learned about it because the secretary happened to be there. Never once did the founder say anything like, "Yes, I cleaned the restroom on a Shinkansen train—I hope that members will also clean those at their Dharma centers, at the very least when they are performing their assigned duties at the centers."

> Even though I may wish for everyone's happiness and make it my job to pray for your happiness, I cannot give you happiness. . . . The happiness you might be feeling today is not something I have given you—it is the joy and well-being that you have achieved through your own effort and continuing religious training, and results from the principle of causation contained in the Buddha Dharma. (*Niwano Nikkyo Howa Senshu* [Selected Dharma Talks of Nikkyo Niwano], vol. 3, p. 356)

What about you and me, what would we do in a similar situation? We would probably consider a dirty restroom a bad encounter, close the door right after opening it, and look for a clean one. If the next one were occupied, we might even go to the next car to find a clean one.

To the founder, however, such an encounter was merely another opportunity to do a good deed "so that the next person can use it without disgust." Because it was dirty, another good deed could be performed. When you encounter an unpleasant situation, you can transform it into a positive one. This is what it means to treasure every encounter and, by means of whatever situation is presenting itself, to cultivate the fields in our hearts and minds. Doing this naturally leads to bodhisattva practice that benefits others.

> When you revere the person next to you and mutually connect up through causes and conditions that are positive ones . . . , and when you make it your job to do whatever you can for society, based on this way of thinking, the next person

and the next one after that will come to find this style of association pleasant, and their spirits will become extremely mellow. (*Gudo* [Search for the Way], December 1976, p. 10)

Only you can cultivate your own spirit. Even though we hope to be happy, we cannot achieve this by ourselves; we need to encounter and relate to other people. Even if you just sit quietly by yourself, you will not be able to cultivate your spirit, nor will you feel joy. When you encounter and relate to another person, your spirit is moved and the raw material and an opportunity for cultivating your spirit come into being. In fact, you cultivate your spirit by dealing with the issues before you, through both joyful and sorrowful events.

For example, when you have to get along with someone who is hard to deal with and you feel you would somehow like to make the person happy, that in itself can be an opportunity for you to cultivate your spirit.

The founder said, "In the society in which we are now living, there cannot be people who are born either good or bad. If your encounters with them are positive ones, they will become good, and if your encounters with them are negative, they will become bad. That is the viewpoint of Buddhism."

One day the founder was making the rounds of Dharma centers and was on his way to a certain one in Tokyo away from the center of the sprawling capital. Though it was his usual practice to arrive for appointments five minutes early, on this particular day he got caught in a traffic jam and ended up arriving thirty minutes late. The faithful, who at first had been joyfully expecting his arrival, had become worn down a bit with waiting and worrying about what might have happened.

The founder's driver was in an even worse state, full of embarrassment and remorse. When the founder arrived, however, he greeted everyone with a big smile and said, "Well, I am very grateful for all that has happened today! Now I understand what you have to go through when you come from some distance to worship at the Great Sacred Hall!"

Hearing this, everyone immediately felt relaxed and happy. They were now rescued. The delay had not been anyone's fault; nobody was going to be criticized, everything had turned out well.

When you can perceive the working of the Buddha in every encounter or event, everything becomes all right. Whenever we seek the Buddha, we are cultivating the fields in our hearts and minds.

> I can expound the Dharma as much as I like, but if nobody is listening, if I have no faithful around me, it will all be for nothing. An encounter with the Dharma causes wonderful spiritual growth in our faithful. They achieve liberation. The fact that our faithful have become liberated (freed from suffering) supports me and enables me to serve as the president. [The founder at this time held the position of president of Rissho Kosei-kai.] This was not because of any virtue in me. This was simply because the Buddha vouchsafed me great virtue in the form of faithful believers. (*Tada Hitasurani* [Only Single-Mindedly], p. 27)

We experience a variety of events every day and encounter various people. Our spirits are moved by these encounters. When our spirits are thus moved, if we, like the founder, express our feelings to others in a warm and friendly way, we are cultivating our spirits.

You are not the only one who can attain buddhahood—everyone around you can also do so and achieve happiness. You are the one who has to do the cultivating, however. It is your spirit, your heart and mind. When you cultivate these things, your internal state will naturally be expressed as warm words and kind deeds.

When you look at others with such a warm, friendly gaze and accept people as they are, that is cultivating the fields in your heart and mind. Isn't that the proper way to honor the legacy of the founder?

> Encounters are a wonderful thing. To treasure the people we encounter, no matter where or when, isn't that the way of life taught by the principle of causation? . . . I never know how many more years I have left to live, so I think I should live every day doing the best work I can, treasuring all my meetings and encounters with other people. (*Kosei Shimbun,* September 7, 1973)

## 29 Treading the Path without Losing Our Way
### *The Four Requisites*

If we follow in the footsteps of Shakyamuni, we will never lose our way on this journey we call life.

—*Niwano Nikkyo Howa Senshu*
(Selected Dharma Talks of Nikkyo Niwano)

Founder Nikkyo Niwano taught us that "you need not worry, because the Buddha is at all times taking care of you. If you do good, you will experience only good encounters, so do not be anxious." He also repeatedly emphasized the importance of the Four Requisites.

The Four Requisites were taught by the Buddha to facilitate our understanding and practice of the teachings of the Lotus Sutra. These are the Four Requisites: to be safeguarded by the buddhas, planting many roots of virtuous deeds, joining the assembly of those resolved to become awakened, and aspiring to liberate all living beings. These four points elucidate the main tenets of the Buddhist faith. Among them, the founder spoke particularly of how the Buddha is constantly with us and of the joy and tranquillity that is awarded to those who have the determination to act upon their faith and do good. He taught us to thoroughly and faithfully continue to do good until we attain the state of tranquillity, where, whatever happens, we will always be all right.

Ever since the day the founder first encountered the Lotus Sutra, he continued every day to follow the Four Requisites to the letter. This was how his absolute faith and strong will to take refuge in the teaching developed and deepened, and this was how he was able to achieve his inner peace and tranquillity without faltering. The founder most likely taught us about the Four Requisites so often because he wanted us to attain a tranquil state of mind that would stay with us no matter what might happen.

> If you can always maintain the feeling that you are being protected by the gods and the buddhas and free yourself from care, no matter where you go in the world, you will be accepted, and should you go here or should you go there, you will be pleasing to the people you meet. (*Gudo* [Search for the Way], April 1976, p. 33)

When Rissho Kosei-kai had just been set up, my grandmother was concerned about the family's daily needs and asked the founder how long he was planning to persevere in his life of faith. He answered her by quoting from the Lotus Sutra, "I shall continue my faith until I hear the voice of the Buddha calling from the sky, 'Excellent, excellent!'"

Some forty years later, in April 1979, the founder was awarded the Templeton Prize for Progress in Religion, often called the "Nobel Prize in the field of religion." In his commemorative acceptance address at the Guildhall in the City of London—his voice briefly choked up with emotion—the founder said, "I interpret the awarding of the Templeton Prize to me as encouragement from God and the Buddha to continue on the path I have followed thus far."

We can imagine what these words meant to the founder. For him, receiving the Templeton Prize must have appeared as evidence indicating approval by the gods and the buddhas that he had correctly put the teaching of the Buddha into practice. It must indeed have seemed like a voice calling from the sky, "Excellent, excellent!"

> The enlightenment of *shravakas,* disciples who hear and follow the Buddha's teaching, and *pratyekabuddhas,* those engaged in religious training without a teacher, is by no means futile, for it is undoubtedly on the right path to true enlightenment, but it is merely partway to the goal. . . . One has only a little further to go. (*Shinshaku Hokke Sambu-kyo* [New Commentary on the Threefold Lotus Sutra], vol. 4, p. 348)

One day a member of Rissho Kosei-kai raised a certain issue with the founder, saying, "A rumor is being widely reported in popular weekly magazines about a prediction that on a certain day of a certain month, some kind of extraordinary natural phenomenon or disaster will happen without fail. And that day is today. I am so worried that something will take place before midnight tonight that I can barely control my feelings."

The founder replied, "I have no power to predict such things. However, I do know how to receive the protection of the gods and the buddhas." He added, "In any event, why don't you try to stay awake until midnight?" He then took his leave with a big smile.

I heard that the upshot was that nothing in any sense extraordinary happened on that day after all.

The person who had brought up the matter later said to me,

"Rather than worry about a day you haven't yet experienced and let predictions and rumors muddle your mind, all you need to do is believe in the protection of the gods and the buddhas. Then, in keeping with the tranquillity you enjoy thanks to that protection, you can carry out the Buddha's wishes. That's all there is to it."

> The joy and self-confidence that come from knowing that you are enjoying the guardianship of the Buddha at all times and in all places can be attained precisely when you are doing good deeds that the Buddha will endorse with his protection. (*Kosei,* March 1966, p. 12)

The most important thing for us is to have faith in the wishes and the protection of the Eternal Original Buddha and to practice the bodhisattva path, the only path that can lead us to attain buddhahood.

We believe that the Buddha is always with us; we join our hearts and hands with fellow members of the sangha and seek to "aspire to liberate all living beings." This is the path that the founder trod and showed to us so that we can follow without getting lost. It is the path to fulfilling the Buddha's most fundamental wish—to bring happiness to all the people of the world.

> To "aspire to liberate all living beings": trying to gain liberation for yourself alone is simply futile and is not in the spirit of the Lotus Sutra. When your heart and mind awaken to the desire to be liberated along with all sentient beings, and when you feel that you would like to bring that liberation to everyone in the entire world and make society a better place, that is what the fourth of the Four Requisites is teaching us. (*San Reizan Meiso* [Meditations from Three Holy Mountains], p. 25)

As a young lad from a mountain village in Niigata Prefecture, the founder came to Tokyo and, putting his faith absolutely in nothing but the words of the Buddha and staking his whole life on that without any form of security, accomplished so much, becoming able to say merely, "I do know how to receive the protection of the gods and the buddhas no matter what happens under any circumstances." It is no easy task to attain the absolute confidence that one will naturally be protected. All we need to do is to take over what the founder left for us and unfalteringly follow on the path he himself trod and showed to us.

I am nobody particularly special. I was just a country boy, an ordinary youth. Thus there is no reason why any of you could not do what I have done. I hope that all of you will resolve right now to start anew and become the people who will lead the new generation. (*Yakushin* [Progress], December 1965, p. 12)

# 30  Be Happy Together, Be as One
## *Many in Body but One in Spirit*

Moving forward together, becoming happier together—because this is the truly humanitarian way to live.

—*Shinshaku Hokke Sambu-kyo*
(New Commentary on the Threefold Lotus Sutra)

In his later years, when requested to "say a few words," Founder Nikkyo Niwano often repeated the statement, "Get along with each other and be one in spirit." This was a rather concise remark from the founder full of years, but I believe it was meant to include the idea that we are all equal in that we are born into this world with the same wish.

The founder also used to say that "even if Buddhism is true, sound, and precious, unless we understand how we need to be united as a group cooperating in pursuit of a common goal, the teachings will not spread. This is why I have always spoken of how we are many in body but one in spirit."

It is usually not possible for a group of individuals with different life circumstances and different ideas to consistently have the same outlook and opinions and act in concert.

However, when we remember that even people with different opinions are all equal in that they all have the same wish of manifesting the buddha-nature within themselves and are born into this world as part of the great Life, this impossibility becomes a possibility. I think a state of "many in body but one in spirit" is achieved when we awaken to this truth.

Once, at a meeting dedicated to interreligious cooperation, despite sincere and heated discussions, opinions remained divided and the participants failed to reach agreement. The founder stood up to deliver the concluding remarks and said, "Today, thanks to all participants, we had a wonderful meeting. Everyone participated wholeheartedly, and that wholehearted zeal was what gave rise to clashes of opinion. I thank you all for your energetic debates and your cooperation."

Just as the group was about to disperse, still in a mood reflecting their lack of agreement, they were suddenly reminded that they had just been furiously debating one another in pursuit of a common purpose.

> When a variety of people are expressing different opinions, those who are listening must be of a mind to truly listen. In a context of interreligious cooperation, this is where Buddhism shines. Buddhist truth can bring about liberation through both "agreement" and "disagreement." In a world such as ours today, the liberation of those who are in disagreement as well as those who are in agreement must be achieved. (*Hosshin* [Raising Aspirations], September 1990, p. 16)

This passage is an expression of the founder's overall view that "all of us are candidates to be buddhas who were born into this world with the same wish" and "all of our lives derive from the same one great Life." Even when people are working together toward a common goal, they will not necessarily adopt the same opinions. However, I think that when there is an awareness that the goal can be the same even though opinions may differ, as the number of people with this awareness increases, the right path toward that goal will inevitably open up.

> I think a state of "many in body but one in spirit" happens only when there is consensus among people, each of whom is continually striving for individual self-realization. (*Kosei,* January 1962, p. 8)

I believe that when the founder spoke of "many in body but one in spirit," he did not mean that "everyone should think alike" but that "all living things are originally manifestations of the one great Life that is the Buddha."

# 31  We All Walk the Great Path Together
## *The Supreme Way*

"May this deed of merit / Extend to all creatures / That we with all the living / May together accomplish the Buddha-way!" This is called "the closing verse of vows" because not only the practitioners of the Lotus Sutra but all believers in Buddhism recite it as a closing verse in their sutra-chanting service. It is said that the spirit of the great vow and practice of Buddhists can be summed up in these few short lines.

*—Buddhism for Today*

After Founder Nikkyo Niwano encountered the Lotus Sutra, he continued for more than sixty years to follow the path laid out by this one scripture. By living this way throughout his life, the founder showed us that our own way of life and mission should be to express through our practical, everyday actions the truth that "we are all children of the Buddha."

Habitually recognizing the working of the Buddha in every encounter is a skill very difficult to obtain. When faced with people and events that we perceive as antagonistic, often we cannot bring ourselves to believe that they may contain the means for our liberation.

It is difficult to discover the Buddha. This is why the Lotus Sutra is considered resistant to belief and understanding. Thus, it is important to start out with faith.

> The gods and the buddhas want to protect us all. Indeed, the "liberation of all" is the Buddha's original vow. To be granted the Buddha's protection, we must follow a path that leads to the fulfillment of that wish. That is why "we all walk on the great path together." (*Hosshin* [Raising Aspirations], January 1989, p. 16)

> "All things depend on faith," and the ability to believe first of all leads to "liberation." We must also not forget "the liberation of others" but continually retain the will to bring about others' liberation and encourage ourselves to be diligent in advancing spiritually. (*Hosshin* [Raising Aspirations], February 1989, p. 16)

At one particular Dharma center, there was a leader who was always dropping off to sleep. Everyone knew she was tired from taking care of her husband's elderly parents. Even so, with everyone striving to carry out practice with hearts united, the other center leaders wondered if there were not some way to get her to stay awake and take an active part.

As recipients of the founder's teaching that draws us toward the great path, how should we respond to this situation? As I am sure you realize, we should warmly accept that the leader was performing the bodhisattva practice at home and, with a feeling of admiration for her efforts, let her sleep. In fact, when everyone in the Dharma center united in a feeling of warm affection for her, sure enough, her situation at home took a turn for the better, and she no longer dozed off during practice.

> The Lotus Sutra is said to be resistant to belief and understanding, but this is also because it teaches the Truth and thus is difficult to understand without the heart of a bodhisattva. (*San Reizan Meiso* [Meditations from Three Holy Mountains], p. 12)

It is best not to worry about these difficulties but simply go ahead and do our best to practice the teaching. We are the ones who create the difficulty, by thinking "This is how things ought to be" rather than recognizing things as they actually are.

Difficulties arise when we try to "solve" problems. We judge certain phenomena to be antagonistic and hard to deal with and thus create troublesome problems for ourselves.

We should concentrate on perceiving the buddha-nature in people and viewing them with warmth and an attitude of Buddhist compassion. That is the great path.

> The way to liberation is simple. Take the lesson of Truth as it comes, believe it, and put it into practice. When you do put it into practice, the supposedly difficult Lotus Sutra becomes comprehensible, and you can directly feel its wonderful qualities. What is most important is to learn from the sutra with an open mind. When you hear that "anyone can attain buddhahood," the best response is to simply take the attitude that says, "That's wonderful! I'd surely like to learn the way to attain buddhahood." (*San Reizan Meiso* [Meditations from Three Holy Mountains], p. 12)

The founder was like a young man throughout his entire life. For the benefit of those who were to come after him, he believed wholeheartedly in the way without end and always continued along that way, thus showing us the joy to be gained walking on the Supreme Way.

In 1994 the Sixth World Assembly of the World Conference of Religions for Peace took place in Italy. The opening ceremony was to be held at the Vatican, and Pope John Paul II had agreed to attend. The founder for many years had been hoping that the pope would attend a Religions for Peace assembly.

However, at this time the founder was nearly ninety years old, and his health was far from perfect. This was very apparent to me as a member of the family on the scene. As his grandchild, all I wanted was to keep my precious grandfather from straining himself. I hoped that somebody else could be chosen to attend in his place. This situation made us all painfully aware that we would have to take up the journey on the path he had shown us if we wanted the founder to relax and rest in a way befitting his age.

I tell you, the path that most people have been following is after all the true path. And that is why we follow it and must teach others to follow that path. We simply have to give a bit of guidance . . . ; these people are following the same path we are. If you start walking by yourself and keep on walking, sooner or later the path will become the true path. (*Hosshin* [Raising Aspirations], December 1986, p. 17)

"Well, I'm on my way, even if it's the last thing I do." Thus saying, the founder left for the Vatican. The expression on his face and the set of his shoulders as he headed out the door remain clearly engraved on my mind to this day. Seeing him at that moment revealed to me that in order to realize the world of the Buddha's enlightenment in our own world, a way exists that we must follow even at the risk of our lives.

It is in achieving the invigorating state of nonself, wherein one is willing to throw away even one's life, that the ever-abiding buddha-nature emerges. (*Shinshaku Hokke Sambu-kyo* [New Commentary on the Threefold Lotus Sutra], vol. 7, p. 153)

Where the founder was going at the risk of his life may not have been a place called the Vatican but rather the world of the Buddha brilliant with light, where all differences between countries and religions have been overcome.

As the founder imparted to us while he was alive, this is "the path that leads to enlightenment" that we can believe in and follow. This is the Supreme Way along which we proceed together.

"We will not love body and life, / But only care for the Supreme Way." What a splendid verse this is. As long as a single person who has not been touched by the supreme teaching remains in the world, we cannot help but feel regret for that. What value can our individual lives have in comparison? Such is the fervent mind-set of one who lives in compassion and in the true Dharma. (*Shinshaku Hokke Sambu-kyo* [New Commentary on the Threefold Lotus Sutra], vol. 6, p. 161)

## 32  Bringing Light to Future Generations
### *Inheritance of the Dharma*

What is most important and what will lead people to the Buddhist faith is, I think, to do exactly what Shakyamuni said, to take the light of Buddhism and communicate it to others in its true form. All we need to do is lay down that single track of light for them.

—*Niwano Nikkyo Howa Senshu*
(Selected Dharma Talks of Nikkyo Niwano)

In June 1982, Founder Nikkyo Niwano, then the president of Rissho Kosei-kai, delivered an address at the Second Special Session of the United Nations General Assembly Devoted to Disarmament (SSD II) in New York. As a Buddhist and a citizen of a country that had suffered the effects of atomic bombings, he called for the abolition of nuclear weapons and declared that Rissho Kosei-kai was ready to take the lead in developing a movement for international disarmament. A special delegation for peace from Rissho Kosei-kai attended this meeting and was listening as the founder spoke.

After the special delegation returned to Japan, a meeting to report on their trip was held at the Great Sacred Hall in Tokyo, and a representative of the youth group said, "Our group is prepared to stand shoulder to shoulder with President Niwano and work for peace," declaring the group's determination with a keen show of emotion.

> The greatest goal young people can have is to realize peace in this world; that is my feeling. Young people have the energy of newly sprouting plants. They are fresh and growing and can carry us up and out of the quagmire of our times. (*Hosshin* [Raising Aspirations], August 1990, pp. 16–17)

Subsequently the youth-group representative was aware that there had been some murmuring to the effect that his choice of the phrase "stand shoulder to shoulder with President Niwano" might have been a little presumptuous. Worried that he might have been in error, the young man took the next opportunity he had to seek guidance from the founder, who told him, "You young people should walk in front of me. That way I can keep my eyes on you and protect you. If you lose your way, I can point out the right road for you," delivering a strong message of encouragement. The young man, impressed by the founder's deep faith and great expectations, found the determination to take an active part in the peace movement.

> When you lay down the track to deliver the light of Buddhism, large numbers of people will quickly gather. People with outstanding qualities will develop, and they will bring the general public along. When you follow such people, you need not fear falling behind. The virtue of laying down a track faithfully in the light of the Buddhist sutras will become

very clear to you. . . . So, to prevent the light of the Buddha's teaching from being cut off, you must constantly hold up the mirror of the Dharma to the eyes of the faithful, right in front of them with nothing blocking the view. This is what we should be striving to do. (*Niwano Nikkyo Howa Senshu* [Selected Dharma Talks of Nikkyo Niwano], vol. 4, p. 276)

Even though you may have been wishing for the happiness of others, sometimes you may feel that you are the one who is falling behind, being passed over, and going unrecognized. The founder has told us that at such times this is not so. "Do not worry. When you feel that you are letting others get ahead, it never needs to mean that you yourself are falling behind." People who put their ego aside to bring the light to others are people who are really able to shine.

We should always be considering how to send the Buddha's light straight into people's hearts. This means properly communicating the Buddhist sutras faithfully, without obscuring their meaning, allowing them to shine appropriately with their own light to one and all. This will allow others to embrace the light. (*Niwano Nikkyo Howa Senshu* [Selected Dharma Talks of Nikkyo Niwano], vol. 4, p. 275)

Life is full of a constant variety of events that call forth from us diverse aspects of our character. When we try to use our encounters with these events, no matter what their nature, as ways to come even a little closer to the warmth of the Buddha in our thoughts and deeds, it means that the light of the Buddha is shining upon us. It is the light that illuminates the path for everyone to attain buddhahood and achieve true happiness, and so we can be serene and happy as we discover the light of the Buddha and walk that path.

> Whether or not you can encounter the Buddha depends first on your having a humble faith, an upright character, and a gentle mind, and on wishing to see the Buddha even at the cost of your life, with a heart that cherishes and longs for the Buddha. That is what we mean by religion, what we mean by faith. (*San Reizan Meiso* [Meditations from Three Holy Mountains], p. 63)

When we encounter problems and suffering, rather than immediately trying to improve things, we should consider whether we can discover any light there. Holding back from searching for some bad cause for the problem, we should instead simply determine to change our lives so we can see everything from then on as either a good cause or a good result. This kind of warm and sincere outlook is like a light that shines on the world, with its never-ending ills and suffering. A world in which all living beings can find liberation starts from that one point of light emanating from a buddha-heart.

> I would like the men and women who will lead this organization in the future to develop the following habit of thought: If they discover something unfavorable to themselves, they consider it as meritorious. Unless they can interpret a negative condition as a positive condition, they will never become religious leaders. . . . That is the type of thinking I use to cope with every event. (*Niwano Nikkyo Howa Senshu* [Selected Dharma Talks of Nikkyo Niwano], vol. 2, p. 352)

## 33 Seeking the Way
### *A Rebirth of Faith*

I was thirty-two years old when I started our organization, and since then I have retained a youthful spirit. I believe I was able to break through the difficulties of that considerable task because I was still relatively young. I hope you, leaders of our youth groups, with your overflowing energy, will take the opportunity presented to you to recognize in Buddhism the true way of liberation and put your hearts and souls into perfecting yourselves and bringing peace to your homes, communities, countries, and the world.

—*Yakushin* (Progress), February 1964

In 1984 Rissho Kosei-kai provided the venue for the World Congress of the International Association for Religious Freedom (IARF) in Tokyo, which was the first such event ever held in Asia. Just two weeks later, the Fourth World Assembly of the World Conference of Religions for Peace took place in Nairobi, Kenya. The founder was entrusted with the ultimate responsibility for both of these major international conferences and spent the months leading up to them traveling to many countries to help solve various difficulties arising as their dates approached. Both of these meetings achieved significant results before successfully coming to a close, and most of the people involved breathed a collective sigh of relief.

At the final press conference at the end of the Kenya event, however, the founder concluded his remarks by saying, "Although I am now nearly eighty years old, I still have the same dream. So let us start again tomorrow on a new journey."

> I established Rissho Kosei-kai because of my great desire to bring practical liberation to people and change the world. It was also because of my conviction that spreading the true spirit of Buddhism as found in the Lotus Sutra was the surest way to actually liberate people and bring change to the world. (*Kosei,* December 1968, p. 7)

It seems to me that the object of the founder's quest was, "How can I bring happiness to this person that I see before me right now, as well as to all people?" For him, that was the single main point.

This single-minded purpose led him to learn about many faiths and ultimately to his encounter with the Lotus Sutra. When this latter occurred, it is said that the founder almost leaped with emotion and exclaimed, "With this, all people can find liberation, every single one!"

However, even after this encounter with the Lotus Sutra, the founder told young people, "My belief is that the spirit of the Lotus Sutra is unsurpassable, but you should find this out for yourself through your own experience. If you encounter any teaching that seems to you more wonderful than the Lotus Sutra, please let me know about it immediately. If I think you are right, I will be happy to join you in your belief right away."

Young people are naturally not yet fully developed. What is important is for them to proceed one step at a time from their youthful ways. Only through making this effort can they discover a way of life that is truly worthwhile. (*Niwano Nikkyo Howa Senshu* [Selected Dharma Talks of Nikkyo Niwano], vol. 4, p. 137)

I think the founder's wish was for everyone to become happy, for all people to find happiness together, and basically that is all that he wanted. In order to accomplish this, he wanted to see the true spirit of the Lotus Sutra spread widely.

For me at this time, to take on of my own volition the founder's dream and his wish for people represents a rebirth of my faith.

While continually seeking the Truth (the Buddha wisdom), nurturing compassion (the Tathagata wisdom), and then aiming for the spirit of true faith (self-existent wisdom), we must strive to carry out our practices in such a way that our buddha-nature comes into full play and that we will then find ourselves in full accord with the mind of the Buddha. (*Shinshaku Hokke Sambu-kyo* [New Commentary on the Threefold Lotus Sutra], vol. 8, p. 209)

Even the smallest thing can help us reach this goal. Discover what is of value in every moment as it goes by. As each day builds upon the day before, we will end up creating a life that has true value and is worth living.

All of we Buddhists serve as the hands and feet of the Buddha; to make the effort needed to realize the Buddha's will in this world and to bring the teaching to life in our everyday actions—that is the aim to which I would like us to devote our energy. (*Niwano Nikkyo Howa Senshu* [Selected Dharma Talks of Nikkyo Niwano], special volume, p. 145)

# Afterword

The founder spent his entire life teaching us what Shakyamuni realized through his enlightenment, which is "to see as light what has always been shining." This world of light is visible everywhere and at all times to all of us—it is only necessary for us to see that it is there.

I would like to be someone who constantly feels the presence of the One Dharma that the founder made his own. I would like to be someone who constantly seeks what the founder sought. And I would like to be someone who constantly feels the warmth and gentle kindness of the Buddha's wish, and one who sees the light of buddha-nature shining in others as a matter of course. I have tried to put these hopes of mine into words.

> The people I see before me now
> Throughout the day that is today,
> Have I seen them as people who have allowed me
> To perform bodhisattva practice
> And further my own growth?

Throughout the day that is today,
Have I been someone bathed in the Buddha's light,
Noticing the buddha-nature and its workings
In myself and in others?

Throughout the day that is today,
Have I been someone who provides hope, joy, and serenity
To anyone who has been with me?

As soon as I was given life in this world, the founder gave me the birth name Mitsuyo, consisting of the kanji characters for *light* (*mitsu*) and *age* or *generation* (*yo*), praying that I would "bring light to the generations to come." At the time of my marriage, my father gave me the Buddhist name Kosho, consisting of the kanji characters for *brightness* (*ko*) and *good omen* (*sho*), praying that I would be "a brilliant omen of good fortune." In order to become someone who can fulfill those prayers and wishes, I hope to walk together with all of you, working together and encouraging each other as we progress along this pathway of light.

My wish is that the light of the teaching that has been given to us by the founder can illuminate for all people the meaning and true value of life. I hope that all who read this book can also communicate that light and see that it shines for the entire world.

With hands held in prayer,
Kosho Niwano